MANCHESTER UNITED'S

PERFECT
10

Sport Media
A Trinity Mirror Business

Sport Media
A Trinity Mirror Business

Published in Great Britain in 2007 by:
Trinity Mirror Sport Media,
PO Box 48, Old Hall Street,
Liverpool L69 3EB

Executive Editor: KEN ROGERS
Art Editor: RICK COOKE
Editorial Assistant: JAMES CLEARY
Cover Design: GLEN HIND

ISBN 978-1905-26630-2

Printed and finished by Brolink

ACKNOWLEDGEMENTS

I would like to dedicate this book to Dr. Peter Welsh and Mr. Ishmail Aldean for the simple reason that without my GP's prompt diagnosis and the surgical brilliance of Trafford's bowel cancer specialist I might well not have been around to write it!

I would also like to acknowledge the contribution of Erik Bielderman and Jean-Philippe Leclaire of *L'Equipe* as well as the interviews my Perfect 10 players have generously afforded me over the years.

It's been good to link up with Trinity Mirror's Ken Rogers again after our years pounding similar football beats in Liverpool and Manchester for our respective papers in our reporting days, and I would also like to express my appreciation for James Cleary's editing work with the book.

ABOUT THE AUTHOR

David Meek has been writing about Manchester United for nearly 50 years after taking over as the *Manchester Evening News* correspondent covering the club in the aftermath of the Munich air tragedy in 1958.

Although retired from the *Evening News* now he has continued to write and broadcast extensively on United and their players, working closely on a number of books with Sir Alex Ferguson as well as co-writing a tribute to the manager marking his 20 years as manager at Old Trafford.

A much-respected commentator on Britain's foremost football club, nobody is better placed to choose a Manchester United Perfect 10 and bring their stories to life.

CONTENTS

Perfect
10

PAGES

United's wall, lining up against Ferencvaros, includes Perfect 10 candidates Stiles, Law, Charlton and Best while (below) another '10', Eric Cantona, is a face in the crowd

Perfect
10

If I am not careful I will be writing more about the players I leave out of my Perfect 10 than I do about the guys I choose. Frankly I am spoilt for choice because Manchester United are the kind of club where successive managers have always been drawn to people who can express themselves, who are good to watch and who are personalities.

Of course playing football is all about winning, but equally important to my mind is how you set about doing it. Are you prepared simply to grind out results? Is the game just a means to an end with winning the sole objective? Or are we also in the entertainment business with flair and style essential components of our teams?

Even Manchester United's fiercest critics would probably concede that down the years Old Trafford has always harboured footballers who cut a dash and who play with a verve and a vision that is good to watch even when the match is lost.

I have certainly found it this way, or I don't think I would be approaching my half-century of reporting, writing and broadcasting the life and times of Manchester United; I would have lost interest by now and found something else to do. As it is, when I set off for Old Trafford I still get the kind of buzz that I enjoyed in my early days as the *Manchester Evening News* reporter after taking over from Tom Jackson in the tragic aftermath of the Munich air crash in February 1958.

Tom had been one of the eight journalists killed in the accident and he himself had obviously found it an enthralling job with 25 years clocked up before his death. Indeed there have only been four Evening News reporters covering Manchester United since Harry P. Renshaw started in 1890 and was presented with a gold watch in 1926 to mark 36 years association with the club. Tom Jackson took over in 1933. My period with the Reds covered 37 years until I retired in 1995 when Stuart Mathieson succeeded me and is looking like a long-server himself. So just four reporters spanning well over a hundred years, and I believe it tells you something about the appeal of Manchester United.

There's something more here than just winning and losing; there's a fascination that makes it difficult to walk away, and for me it's an appeal linked with a tradition for cultivating players who are special with so many of them artists capable of rendering football at its finest.

Manchester United have always been known for their individual stars, players of character who made a difference like Billy Meredith, the toothpick-chewing Welsh winger, who was a key man in United's first successful era when they won the League Championship in 1908 and 1911 along with the FA Cup in 1909. Meredith can claim to have been one of the first celebrity footballers to grace the game and he was certainly on the news pages as well as the sporting back page when he helped to form the Players' Union in defiance of the Football League.

Charlie Roberts was another famous player from those early days and a founder of the Players' Union who led his team-mates out on a strike to train on their own. They called themselves 'The Outcasts' and stayed away from the ground until their Union was officially recognised. Roberts was part of a powerful half-back line that also featured Duckworth and Bell, and if supporters in this era had been asked to nominate their best players there is no doubt that they would have been strong contenders.

There was certainly no more popular figure between the two world wars than another half-back, Joe Spence, a player so loved by the fans that if a performance needed enlivening then the chant would go round the terraces: 'Give it to Joe.' So by the time Sir Matt Busby arrived as manager at the end of the Second World War Manchester United fans had already been introduced to some colourful individual stars.

Once Busby was in his stride the characters certainly came thick and fast as United won the FA Cup in 1948 and the First Division Championship in 1952. Men back from service in the war made up the team of that period and any number of them qualified to be considered among Manchester United's greatest players.

To start with they had a forward line that wasn't called the 'Famous Five' for nothing with Jimmy 'Brittlebones' Delaney on the right wing, Jack Rowley the Gunner at centre-forward, Johnny Morris and Stan Pearson the inside forwards, while Charlie Mitten, the 'Bogata Bandit' who defected to South America, entertained from the left wing. The personalities didn't stop in the attack, not with big Allenby Chilton at centre-half and the side captained by the genial pipe-smoking Johnny Carey who played every position bar goal for them.

Then came the Busby Babes and Old Trafford was flooded with hugely talented players who blended into a team that was beginning to dominate English football until the tragic disaster of the Munich air crash.

Although the accident undoubtedly added an air of mystique, by the time of Munich the Babes had made an immense impact and there is a case to be made for allowing them to take over the Perfect 10.

They were a young and vivacious team with personality bubbling through every position. Nobody was more respected than the captain, left-back Roger Byrne, but the man who dominated at that time was undoubtedly Duncan Edwards, a Colossus always described by Busby assistant Jimmy Murphy as the greatest. Murphy's big responsibility was to oversee the development of the young players, and the tragedy of the Munich air crash meant that right up until his own death he couldn't bear to mention the name of Edwards without tears springing to his eyes. Edwards was part of an extraordinarily gifted group that scored goals for fun through the dashing centre-forward Tommy Taylor and forwards like Dennis Viollet, Billy Whelan, Bobby Charlton, David Pegg, Johnny Berry, Kenny Morgans and Albert Scanlon.

Eddie Colman in midfield was dubbed 'Snake Hips' because of the delightful way he could shimmy his way past opponents and it's with the Babes that I intend to start naming my Perfect 10.

I have decided to begin at this point in the club's history because it enables me to make it a personal selection from players I have seen in action myself. So out of the reckoning must go the stalwart band that brought Busby his first honours as manager. I interviewed most of them in later life, and a jolly interesting bunch they were too with tall tales to tell, like Charlie Mitten who once scored three penalties in a 7-0 win against Aston Villa. He hit the left-hand stanchion with the first two and then in an effort to put him off, Joe Rutherford, the Villa goalkeeper, asked him where he was going to put the third one.

"Same place," said Charlie, which he duly did, so accurate was he with his trusty left foot, but the keeper still couldn't do anything about it!

Charlie made the headlines when he turned rebel and signed for Santa Fe in Colombia to earn what was then a small fortune. Indeed he wrote his own book *The Bogata Bandit* and I would have loved to have included him in my top 10, but I never saw him play.

I did see Duncan Edwards in action, though, and watching from the Maine Road terraces, I will never forget the sight of his majestic figure in that titanic European Cup tie against Bilbao in February of 1957. United had come home from Spain with a 5-3 defeat and even the most loyal of United fans didn't really give them much of a chance of pulling the tie out of the fire.

But with the Busby Babes you just couldn't be sure and there were 70,000 packed into the Manchester City ground to watch what they knew would take a major effort to overturn the deficit. Their faith was well rewarded with goals from Johnny Berry, Tommy Taylor and Dennis Viollet backed with a Herculean display by Duncan Edwards.

I had not long crossed the Pennines to join the *Manchester Evening News* and I have got to say that even though I had thrilled to the efforts of York City on an exciting run to the semi-finals of the FA Cup in 1955, I was gobsmacked by my introduction to football as played by Manchester United. I had certainly never seen a player like Edwards, truly a Colossus, and so that's where I'll start my list of super heroes.

I also feel that by starting my selection from the Busby Babes period I am sharing in the spirit of this year's UEFA celebration of the golden jubilee of the European Union and the 50-year involvement of Manchester United in European football. United beat a Europe XI managed by Marcello Lippi 4-3 at Old Trafford on March 13, 2007, in a game staged to mark this double anniversary, and as my thoughts flew back to the birth of United's great European adventure I thought how appropriate it would be to launch my book with the invincible Edwards.

It would be easy to get sucked into including at least half the Busby Babes because they were a fantastic team and even if you strip away the emotional background of the Munich disaster most judges would acknowledge that before the crash they had had the world of football at their feet. Matt Busby must have felt like me whenever he picked a side…spoilt for choice: Mark

Jones or Jackie Blanchflower for centre-half, Billy Whelan or John Doherty or latterly Bobby Charlton for inside right, David Pegg or Albert Scanlon for outside left, Johnny Berry or Kenny Morgans at outside right.

Dennis Viollet, who survived Munich to score 32 League goals in season 1959-60, still holds the record as United's top scorer in a season. How can I leave him out? Well it's a near thing but there are so many good players to come in the next half-century that Duncan Edwards must represent the pre-Munich period and speak on behalf of a splendid bunch of young athletes.

Sir Matt is mobbed by (left to right) Albert Quixall, Noel Cantwell, Pat Crerand and Tony Dunne following the 1963 FA Cup final victory over Leicester City

We have to wait a while for the next batch of superstars, something that was inevitable after the devastation wrecked by Munich, but it was well worth the wait. In fact considering that Busby had virtually to rebuild from scratch it was amazing that it took him only 10 years to put together the side that took the Sixties by storm with that superlative football trinity of Bobby Charlton, Denis Law and George Best.

We didn't know how spoilt we were at the time to be able to watch three European Footballers of the Year play in the same team at the same time.

It's unique and at the time I'm afraid we rather took it for granted, which is all the more reason why I have no hesitation redressing the balance by including all three in my Perfect 10. In fact it seems everyone is now rushing to pay tribute to a trio of players whose names trip off the tongue like a litany. At the time of writing Manchester United are planning a sculpture by Philip Jackson that will stand outside Old Trafford in much the same way as Sir Matt Busby's bronze stature gazes towards his adopted city of Manchester. Three players, different in styles but united by peerless talent, and they will represent the period that saw Manchester United become the first English club to win the European Cup with that magnificent performance against Benfica at Wembley in 1968.

Sir Bobby Charlton, knighted for his exemplary services to football, was the man who imaginatively and so expressively described Old Trafford as the theatre of dreams in an interview, many years ago, with the late Geoffrey Green of *The Times*.

Denis Law, the original warrior king, is an automatic choice. Only Denis could find TWO books coming out about him at the same time, which is what happened last year, one by himself and the other by admiring fan Brian Hughes. Both were titled *The King*. What else!

George Best completes the threesome, as befits a footballer whose funeral last year triggered such an outpouring of emotion and love from fans all over the country. He is still quite the most magical footballer I have ever seen.

There will be one more chosen from that side, not perhaps blessed with quite the same degree of individual talent, but who for me did more than most to glue all the major personalities together. I'm talking here of Nobby Stiles, an untidy player in many ways but a players' player. Every team needs one, with Sir Alf Ramsey as appreciative as Sir Matt Busby of the worth of a player like Nobby.

And if you think there is a personal bias here, then you're right. I have such admiration for his wholehearted nature, and selfless play, but if you want more definite evidence of his right to be included in what is after all a very distinguished group then I simply point out that only two English footballers hold both a World Cup and European Cup winner's medal, and that's Nobby along with his pal, Bobby Charlton. End of argument.

The European success brought the retirement of Busby and slowly but surely the break-up of that great side. Managers came and went as United fought for a return to the great days. It was not a period with many trophies but there were some outstanding players like Martin Buchan, the legacy of Frank O'Farrell's luckless reign as manager. Tommy Docherty also provided us with some attractive performers who figured in the FA Cup even if they couldn't find the consistency for a League Championship, players like Steve Coppell, Gordon Hill, Stuart Pearson and Jim Holton…'Six foot two, eyes of blue, big Jim Holton's after you.'

Ron Atkinson also revelled in the FA Cup and for four or five years also had his teams finishing in the top four without being able to go all the way. One reason for the consistency of his teams was the inspired signing of Bryan Robson from West Bromwich Albion. They didn't call him Captain Marvel for nothing, as you will discover when you read about the way he defied his body to become the iron man of the game.

His successor at Old Trafford, Roy Keane, was another inspirational captain and as driving midfielders I felt I had to choose between them to join the Perfect 10. Bryan's heroic deeds for England tipped the balance. Roy didn't really flourish on the international stage and it was Sir Alex Ferguson who helped make my mind up when he told me: "Roy was the most influential captain I ever had, but Bryan was the best because he could make decisions out on the pitch in a game and that's priceless for a manager watching helplessly from the sidelines. Bryan could also chip in with around 15 goals a season which from midfield is also a big help!" Bryan didn't share in as many prizes as Roy but that wasn't his fault and he certainly played his part in the Premier League title triumph in 1993, and the League and Cup Double success of 1994 before his time ran out.

Then comes the man who was the right player in the right place at the right time, the catalyst who finally sparked United into Championship-winning form after a frustrating 26 years without being able to win the League.

Eric Cantona's name is still chanted around the ground and it's 12 years since his infamous kung-fu kick at Crystal Palace that had the game in such an uproar. How did 'Oo ah Cantona' originate? United songster Peter Boyle says that when Irishman Paul McGrath played at Old Trafford the fans used to sing 'Oo ah McGra', a chant stolen by Leeds United fans when Cantona arrived at Elland Road and adapted to the Frenchman's name. It goes better, too, and when Sir Alex signed him from Leeds for a giveaway £1m the chant not only came with him but it stuck and continues to this day.

Some might argue that David Beckham's skills as a footballer fall short of what is required to join the Perfect 10 and they might be right, but how can I ignore a personality, an icon, a player who became a celebrity so big that Sir Alex Ferguson thought he was a distraction from the core business of actually playing football. They were on a collision course, particularly since he also suspected that David had also begun to fancy the life of a 'Galatico' in Spain. The outcome was that the United manager shipped David out to Real Madrid, but nobody four years later who heard David's delayed but heartfelt farewell to United supporters during the interval of the UEFA jubilee match at Old Trafford could doubt that Manchester United and indeed Ferguson held a special place in his affections; listening to his reception there could be little doubt either that 'Becks' still has a place in the hearts of United fans. David Beckham is simply too big a figure in the history of Old Trafford to pass over.

If you prefer your footballers to be a little less colourful, a little shyer of publicity and one who prefers the quiet life then you will find your ideal in my next choice, Ryan Giggs, like David, a successful graduate from the FA Youth Cup-winning team of 1992, but in terms of personality as different as chalk and cheese.

Ryan is enjoying a new lease of life after winning a stack of honours with United, and is unspoilt. He has served the club so well, he is exciting to watch and you couldn't put it better than his manager when he says: "Every father would be proud to have a son like Ryan Giggs."

I feel embarrassed at omitting team-mates like Gary Neville and Paul Scholes because they are also terrific home-grown one-club players who represent the heart of the club. When Gary Neville kissed his club badge to celebrate a goal at Liverpool, it wasn't just an extravagant gesture, you knew he meant it. But there's not room for everyone and Ryan Giggs will be their representative as someone who maintains the traditions of a very special club.

I have not been able to find a place either for a goalkeeper, despite Manchester United being particularly strong in this department with men like the steady Jack Crompton who returned to the club as the trainer after Munich to help in the rebuilding, the brave and brilliant Harry Gregg, the popular Alex

Stepney remembered for his great save against Eusebio in the final of the European Cup, and then of course the mighty Peter Schmeichel, the great Dane foundation for the unique treble in 1999. But they don't sprinkle the stardust over goalkeepers in the way they do with attacking players, and so last man in is something of a gamble because nobody knows for sure just how long he will stay at Manchester United.

Never before, though, has a player made such an impact in such a short time. Cristiano Ronaldo has set the pulses of everyone associated with United racing with the way he has taken dribbling skills to a new level. There were a lot of world stars on parade in Marcello Lippi's team in the European celebration match at Old Trafford but the eye-catching performer on the night wore a red shirt.

Wayne Rooney might well have the last laugh as he develops his own prodigious talents, but picking on form I have got to go for the Portuguese youngster described by Lippi after the match: "Ronaldo is a great player with genius and imagination and great technical skills."

I might add that he has tremendous courage, too, and though it's early days yet, for me he is just the man to complete my Perfect 10.

In the eighties, I had my first stab at selecting my personal *Manchester United Greats*, which is always subjective. This latest "Perfect 10" challenge has given me the chance to review my original manuscript and while some things haven't changed, this book will once again spark intrigue amongst the fans while re-igniting the great debate. I hope you enjoy it.

David Meek

1953-1958

Duncan Edwards

Manchester United lost a fine footballer and a majestic man in the Munich air disaster of February 6, 1958. Duncan was only 21, cut down before he was even in his prime, but such had been his impact on the game that he was already being regarded as one of England's truly great players.

Eight years after the crash, England won the World Cup. It might have been sooner had not Roger Byrne, Tommy Taylor and Duncan Edwards, not to mention David Pegg and Eddie Colman, been among the eight players, three United staff, eight journalists, two crew and two other passengers who all perished as their plane failed to take off at the third attempt following a refuelling stop on their way home from a European Cup quarter-final tie against Red Star Belgrade in Yugoslavia.

Duncan fought for his life in Munich's Rechts der Isar Hospital for 15 days after he had been dragged clear from the runway carnage, but his injuries had been massive.

His performances for both club and country had caught the imagination of the whole country and the football world lay at his feet with the promise of so much to come when he was caught up in the maelstrom of Munich.

He had already won 18 caps and after captaining the England Schoolboy team and the U23 side, was regarded as the natural successor to Billy Wright at senior level.

He had been the youngest to play for England when he was

given his first cap in April 1955, at the age of 18 years and eight months, incidentally a debut marked by beating Scotland at Wembley 7-2. It was England's biggest win over the Scots in a peacetime fixture.

Walter Winterbottom, the England manager of that era, had no doubts about the player's international worth when he said: "Duncan was a great footballer and he had the promise of being the greatest of his day. He played with tremendous joy and his spirit stimulated the whole England team. It was in the character and spirit of Duncan Edwards that I saw the true revival of British football."

Jimmy Armfield, who went on to captain England himself and who also played with Duncan during National Service in the Army, claims: "With Duncan in the team I believe England would have at least reached the final of the 1958 World Cup.

"The first thing that struck you was his enormous build. He almost had the physique of a weight lifter and certainly when he played against people in his own age group he appeared to carry almost twice their strength.

"Playing in the same team together I can still see this powerful figure stalking the dressing room and at the time I would think: 'I'm glad he's playing for us.'

"But it wasn't just power that made him a first-class player. He had highly-skilled techniques. He was a brilliant footballer who never thought about losing. He was the perfect footballer, one of the finest all-round players I ever saw, or am ever likely to see. He deserves to be what he is, a football legend."

His shooting was eye-catching, too, and even impressed the Germans. His shots had packed so much power when he had played in England's 3-1 win in Germany that when Manchester United landed in West Berlin a few months later for the start of a pre-season tour, German fans were calling for 'Boom Boom.'

Duncan was born in Dudley near Wolverhampton and first came to attention playing for the Dudley Boys team. Bt the time he was captaining the England schoolboy side the whole football world had heard of him, not least Stan Cullis, who naturally had him earmarked for Molineux, and the Wolves manager was not best pleased when Matt Busby came calling as he recruited the youngsters who would go on to become the Busby Babes.

United had a trump card in the competition to sign this outstanding boy, as became clear when United heard that Wolves were about to step in for him. United's scout in the Midlands put in a hurried call to Old Trafford and Matt immediately dispatched his coach Bert Whalley to the Edwards home.

Although it was long past bedtime Bert knocked the family up and Duncan came downstairs in his pyjamas to ask what all the fuss was about. "I've already said Manchester United are the only club I want to join," he said.

Duncan duly signed a schoolboy form but that only triggered the suspicion that United must have paid money to get him to Manchester. Busby insisted that the explanation was much simpler. "The boy simply wanted to play for Manchester United," he explained.

Busby later told the story: "I remember one particularly great display by Duncan on the Wolves ground and there was a big inquest on Duncan in the board room after the match. Stan Cullis said to me: 'Matt, I'd just like to know how you managed to sign Edwards because we thought he was all lined up to join us.' I told Stan that we got him in the same way he had signed Colin Booth, a Manchester boy. Colin was supposed to be joining Manchester United and I was actually with his parents the night before he signed for Wolves. It was simply a case of him just wanting to go to Wolves. In the same way Duncan wanted to play for United."

Duncan arrived at Old Trafford just as the FA Youth Cup was being launched for season 1952-53 and he was an obvious and immediate selection. Indeed, he played a major role establishing United as the early masters of the competition with United winning the FA Youth Cup for five successive seasons from its inception.

Duncan played in the first three and ironically in the inaugural season United met Wolves in the final – and beat them 9-3 over the two legs. No wonder Stan Cullis never really forgave United for 'stealing' him from under their noses, and to rub salt into the wound United again met Wolves in the final the following year. This time Duncan Edwards scored twice in a 5-4 aggregate win.

By the time of his third season in the FA Youth Cup Duncan Edwards had become a regular in the first team but he liked nothing better than to turn out with his contemporaries and he was brought back for the final against West Bromwich Albion when he was conspicuous in a crushing 7-1 win over two legs.

At this level he was a veritable tank and almost unstoppable. In one tie at Chelsea, Jimmy Murphy, in fairness to the rest of the team, gave pre-match instructions that they should remember it was a team game and that they should play without undue reliance on Edwards. At half-time they were a goal down so he told them to forget his earlier instruction and look to give Duncan the ball. They did and he scored twice for a 2-1 win!

In another youth game, playing at Charlton, Edwards was having a relatively quiet time and one Cockney near the dugout kept giving Jimmy stick about his star youngster. "We ain't seen him, mate," he shouted, but even as he spoke Edwards rocketed in a goal from 40 yards and a delighted Murphy turned round to say: "There, my friend, is Duncan Edwards."

Jeff Whitefoot and Duncan Edwards were the first of the Babes to break into the first team. Both were still playing in the youth side but around this time Busby was ready to give youth a fling. He gave Duncan his debut against Cardiff City at Old Trafford on April 4th, 1953, at the tender ago of 16 and 185 days, though this is not a record, despite a widely held belief that it is. The distinction of being United's youngest in League football belongs to Jeff Whitefoot who was 16 and 105 days when he had made his senior bow against Portsmouth some three years earlier.

Duncan's debut was marked by a 4-1 defeat and he didn't play again that season. The following year, though, he strode majestically into action as Sir Matt began to unveil more of his multi-talented Busby Babes, the youngsters who quickly started to sweep all before them. It was the beginning of a short but sweet golden age as the manager began to break up the team of war veterans who had won the FA Cup in 1948 and the Championship in 1952.

Matt was itching to give his boys, 'the acorns', as Jimmy Murphy used to put it (who were fast growing into oak trees) their head, and the decisive moment came on October 31, 1953. He brought in Duncan Edwards along with Dennis Viollet and Jackie Blanchflower to replace some of the old guard like Stan Pearson, Henry Cockburn and Harry McShane for a League match at Huddersfield. Bill Foulkes and Jeff Whitefoot had already forced their way into the side while David Pegg joined the newcomers before the end of the season.

The following year saw Mark Jones, Albert Scanlon and Billy Whelan promoted to complete the Babes' takeover and provide the basis for the Championship success of season 1955-56. The one gatecrasher from outside was Tommy Taylor, the rampaging centre forward bought for £29,999 from Barnsley, but he was also young and fitted into Busby's home-spun team as if he had been there all his life.

Taylor led the title charge with 25 goals while Viollet scored 20. Duncan Edwards had played as an inside forward in his early days in the senior side but in the Championship year he settled into his best position at left-half and he was a powerhouse unleashed. He wasn't the giant, as he was sometimes described, because he wasn't particularly tall, under 6ft in fact. His legs and chest were what made him powerful.

The title team with Duncan Edwards making 33 League appearances and scoring three goals at No 6, mostly lined up:

Wood, Foulkes, Byrne, Whitefoot or Colman, Jones, Edwards, Berry, Doherty or Whelan, Taylor, Viollet, Pegg.

Jackie Blanchflower, Colin Webster and Ian Greaves also enjoyed spells in a side that took the title by storm to finish 11 points in front of second-placed Blackpool. Their average age was barely 22…Babes indeed with Duncan Edwards typifying the spirit and style of a team ready to tackle anything, including Europe!

Matt Busby, a visionary who saw football as a global game, had a natural ambition to pit his talented team against the best that Europe could produce and he encouraged Manchester United to defy the Football League and accept an invitation to represent England in the European Champions Cup.

His confidence was hardly misplaced. Edwards missed the opening game against Anderlecht in Belgium through injury but he was back in the side for the second leg played at Manchester City because Old Trafford didn't have floodlights.

United ran up a staggering 10-0 victory. Jeff Mermans, their captain and a distinguished Belgian international, conceded: "After United had scored their sixth goal, they still ran as hard as they had at the start. We have played against the best teams of Hungary and Russia and never been beaten like this. Why don't they pick this team for England?" he asked.

The line-up for the historic match in Manchester was:

Wood, Foulkes, Byrne, Colman, Jones, Edwards, Berry, Whelan, Taylor, Viollet, Pegg.

The Welsh referee, Mervyn Griffiths, joined in the tributes and said: "I have never seen football more deadly in execution."

But though everyone at Old Trafford, including the supporters, had been thrilled by the quality of the football and the overwhelming score line, the ripples of the victory were far more significant. For a start, the decision to enter the European Cup had been vindicated. The domestic fixtures had been completed on time and there had been no problems involved in a midweek flight abroad. There was no possibility of recrimination from the Football League. They had answered all the questions and there were none left for the League to pose.

Even more importantly perhaps was the feel-good factor that United had brought back for English football after the disappointment of the national team, twice humiliated by the Hungarians who had even beaten England 6-3 at Wembley. At last football followers, and not just United fans, had a team to be proud of and worthy of allegiance.

This was undoubtedly one of the early factors that saw Manchester United become immensely popular. It was a team for all, with Duncan Edwards emerging as the kind of sporting inspiration capable of becoming a national hero, as well as a United star, if he wasn't already.

The early days in Europe created a special glamour and stature which was to see United become the best-known and widest supported English club through the years since, even during those periods when there was an absence of trophies!

A fuse had been lit and had certainly caught the imagination of the Manchester public because for the next round and a visit from Borussia Dortmund, an incredible 75,598 squeezed into the Manchester City ground. The Germans were beaten 3-2 before a goalless draw in Dortmund.

The quarter-final saw the Babes thrill the nation by coming back from the tricky situation of losing 5-3 against Athletic Bilbao in Spain to win 3-0 in Manchester for an aggregate victory that took them into the semi-finals against mighty Real Madrid.

United lost 3-1 in Madrid, but Edwards still managed to stand out with 'Old International', *The Guardian's* football writer who would also lose his life in the Munich air crash, referring to the "oak-tree strength of Edwards."

United played valiantly in the return for a 2-2 draw at Old Trafford, and so out they went on aggregate, but they had been up against the best team in Europe and as Busby summed up, Real Madrid's vast experience made the difference.

For a first-time campaign in Europe, though, it had been an inspiring effort and clearly there was so much more to come from Busby's young side with talented players like Duncan Edwards just on the cusp of their careers.

The introduction of the Busby Babes had been no flash in the pan because in addition to their brilliant handling of their first European campaign they proceeded to win the League again, this time romping home to the Championship eight points ahead of Spurs with the team now settling into a line-up of:

Wood, Foulkes, Byrne, Colman, Jones, Edwards, Berry, Whelan, Taylor, Viollet, Pegg.

Their scoring topped the ton with the help of 26 from Billy – Liam in his native Ireland – Whelan, 22 by Tommy Taylor and 16 from Dennis Viollet. The season was also notable for the introduction of yet another youngster, Bobby Charlton, who made a name for himself by scoring 10 goals from 14 appearances.

Duncan Edwards made 34 League appearances and scored five goals in a superb half-back line that provided the perfect balance with the power of Duncan on the left in contrast to the silky skills of Eddie Colman, dubbed 'snake hips' because of his beautiful dribbling skills, on the other flank.

United also enjoyed a run in the FA Cup that season with Edwards the hero in the fifth round when he scored to give the Reds a 1-0 win against Everton at Old Trafford.

The League title was already in the bag when United walked out for the final at Wembley against Aston Villa as firm favourites to complete a League and FA Cup Double. In fact Matt Busby told me in later years that when he walked down the stairs of their hotel on the morning of the final that he had never been more sure of winning a football match.

What he didn't know of course was that the Villa striker, Peter McParland, would career into Ray Wood and leave the United goalkeeper concussed and with a broken cheekbone …and this after just six minutes with no substitutes, not even for the goalkeeper, allowed.

Wood was helped off with Jackie Blanchflower taking over in goal and Duncan Edwards switched to centre-half. The 10 men did well and Tommy Taylor headed a fine goal, but Wembley is no place for a team a man short and they couldn't prevent the rampant McParland twice breaking through to score for a 2-1 win.

Towards the end Busby gambled by sending Wood back on and the players responded by recapturing some of their usual rhythm but not even Edwards could turn the tide.

So that was the end of the League and FA Cup Double dream but with two championships and a Cup final appearance under their belt as well as a decent debut in Europe the excitement around Old Trafford was electric.

Duncan Edwards was also outstanding with England of course, though international football always posed a problem for his mentor at Old Trafford, Jimmy Murphy, who was manager of Wales as well as Sir Matt Busby's assistant responsible for the development of the young players.

Before one particular England-Wales match, Jimmy was running through the opposition detailing strengths and weaknesses. He referred to every England player bar Edwards which left Reg Davies, the Welsh and Newcastle inside forward, feeling a little neglected, especially as he was in direct opposition to the United and England wing-half.

"What about Edwards?" queried Davies. Replied Murphy: "There's nothing I could say which would help us. Just keep out of his way, son!"

Murphy regarded Duncan Edwards as simply the greatest and up to the time of his own death could barely mention Duncan's name without a tear coming to his eye.

Jimmy poignantly recalled in his book *United, Matt and Me*: "Duncan was the Kohinoor diamond among our crown jewels, the greatest of them all. If I shut my eyes I can see him now. Those pants hitched up, the wild leaps of boyish enthusiasm as he came running out of the tunnel, the tremendous power of his tackle – always fair but fearsome – the immense power on the ball.

"In fact, the number of times he was robbed of the ball once he had it at his feet could be counted on one hand. He was a players' player. Ask Bobby Charlton and he will tell you Duncan was the greatest.

"When I hear Mohammed Ali proclaim on television and radio that he is the greatest I have to smile, because there was only ever one and that was Duncan Edwards.

"Any manager lucky enough to have him had half a team. And that is why, when I heard the sad news of Duncan's death on the morning of Friday, February 21, 1958, I broke down and cried. The club and England had lost a great footballer. I had lost a friend, a very dear friend.

"From the first time I saw him as a boy of 14, he looked like and played with the assurance of a man, with legs like tree trunks, a deep and powerful chest and an unforgettable zest for the game. He played wing-half, centre-half, centre-forward and inside forward with the consummate ease of a great player. He

was never bothered where he played. He was quite simply a soccer Colossus."

Sir Bobby Charlton was certainly another admirer and he knew Duncan well after spending part of their National Service together in the same Army unit, as well as playing with him for both club and country of course.

He told me: "I am not being disrespectful to the others but Duncan Edwards was the best. He was a passionate footballer. I speak about him so often but he had the lot. He was our talisman and he was made for European football.

"I see him in my mind's eye and wonder that anyone should have so much talent."

Bobby recalls in his book *My Soccer Life*: "We were 4-2 down with the game nearly over so Duncan switched to centre forward. In 10 minutes he scored four and we won 7-4.

"I quote that example of him in a relatively unimportant match because I think it supplies a key to his genius. For Duncan, you see, there was no such thing as an unimportant match. In one season he played nearly a hundred games for United, England and the Army – and he gave 100 per cent in the lot.

"I don't say he intended to. There were probably small-time Army games when he thought he would have a quiet cruise through – just keep out of trouble and not over-tire himself for the next international or League match. But once the game started everything else went out of his mind. He ran and tackled and surged through as if his reputation depended upon it. Whether it was at Wembley or on a bumpy pitch behind the barracks, he became immersed in it."

Bobby remembers when he first joined United and met Jimmy Murphy for the first time. His new coach apparently talked non-stop about the attributes of a fellow called Edwards.

"I wondered why he was bothering with me if this Edwards was so good. Later I understood why Jimmy couldn't stop talking about him. Duncan was the greatest. He had the sort of build a boxer pines for. He was a shade under six feet and weighed about 13-and-a-half stone. He was a hard, tough man in the tackle, but he was also a shrewd, intelligent player.

"His other exceptional quality was that he always liked to be winning or saving matches. He had a shot that could burst through the best goalkeeper's hands, yet when the pressure was on in his own goalmouth, he would be back there battling away.

"He had the sort of speed that made that possible and ensured he was never caught out of position. One minute he would be clearing off his line, the next surging through at the other end. He was out on his own at left-half, and a First Division player in every other position."

United started season 1957-58 in good shape and full of confidence after winning the Championship for a second successive season, reaching the semi-final of the European Cup at their first attempt and playing in the final of the FA Cup. They had everything going for them with a stunning, free-scoring attack, a resolute defence and a fantastic half-back line featuring Duncan Edwards, who was so good that he kept the former England schoolboy captain Wilf McGuinness out of the side, and Wilf, already an England U23 international, was a good player.

Busby even had more talented youngsters breaking through like Albert Scanlon, Kenny Morgans and Alex Dawson. United had a squad that was young and deep in quality and they launched into the new season in good heart with every expectation of even more success.

They won five of their first six games and drew the other, scoring not less than three goals in every match for a total of 22 to measure up to their billing as the great entertainers. Duncan Edwards was naturally in the thick of it scoring six goals and missing only two games before the fateful European Cup quarter-final second leg against Red Star Belgrade in Yugoslavia.

His last game on English soil was in the spectacular 5-4 League victory against Arsenal at Highbury which somehow represented everything Manchester United stood for in the game, classic football played with flair and commitment. Duncan scored a typical goal to give United the lead and with further goals by Bobby Charlton and Tommy Taylor they led 3-0 at half-time, only for Arsenal to stage a tremendous fight-back that saw them level the score at 3-3.

The scene was set for a thrilling and dramatic finish as Edwards and company stepped up a gear to win 5-4 with a goal from Dennis Viollet and another from Taylor.

If a football epitaph was needed to express the power and the glory of the 21-year-old Duncan Edwards and his young team-mates, then it was unforgettably etched at Highbury that day.

The team lined up:

Gregg, Foulkes, Byrne, Colman, Jones, Edwards, Morgans, Charlton, Taylor, Viollet, Scanlon.

Jack Kelsey, the Arsenal goalkeeper said: "It was the finest match I ever played in, and in Duncan Edwards, Manchester United had a player with all the promise in the world. Even in the conditions that day – ankle deep mud – his strength stood out. He was a Colossus."

That season along with their impressive League form, they had again produced a storming campaign in Europe, opening with a convincing 6-0 win over Shamrock Rovers in Dublin in the first leg of the preliminary round. Matt Busby made one or two changes for the home leg, leaving out Duncan Edwards and Billy Whelan in order to give players like Wilf McGuinness and Colin Webster a game. They were still too strong for the Irish part-timers, though, and they eased through 3-2 at Old Trafford before taking on sterner opposition in Dukla Prague.

United won 3-0 in Manchester, good enough to come through on aggregate after going down 1-0 in the second leg in Czechoslovakia.

Now they were through to the quarter-final to meet Red Star Belgrade, a tougher challenge, but they were at full strength and with goals from Bobby Charlton and Eddie Colman they won the first leg at Old Trafford 2-1. The team were flying now and four days later with the help of a goal from Edwards and a hat-trick from Bobby Charlton, they thrashed Bolton 7-2 at Old Trafford.

Then they shared in the Highbury extravaganza before turning their thoughts back to Europe and flying out for what they knew would be a searching second leg in Belgrade

Boosted by the plaudits that had been handed them for their stylish display at Arsenal, they sailed into a three-goal half-time lead with two goals from Bobby Charlton and one from Dennis Viollet. They were 5-1 up on aggregate and the match looked to be over, but two minutes into the second half Red Star pulled a goal back and then got another with a penalty. Now the Yugoslavs had their tails up and they hammered away at Harry Gregg in the United goal.

With just four minutes remaining Gregg came running to the edge of the box to take a threatening cross only to stumble and fall outside the area. Kostic bent the free-kick round him to draw level on the night and now Red Star needed just one more goal to draw level on aggregate. Somehow the Reds hung on to qualify for the semi-finals for the second year running.

The last line-up for the Busby Babes read:

Gregg, Foulkes, Byrne, Colman, Jones, Edwards, Morgans, Charlton, Taylor, Viollet, Scanlon.

It was the last match for the cream of the country's top football writers as well as for so many of the Busby Babes.

George Follows of the *Daily Herald*, one of those who perished, described the match as the best football he had ever seen Manchester United play, while Tom Jackson, my predecessor who had reported on United for 25 years, didn't live to appreciate that Tom Henry, his editor, had made his report and photograph of the last line-up the page one lead in the *Manchester Evening News*.

On the international front, Bobby Robson had made his England debut in what was to prove Duncan's last game for England, a 4-0 win against France at Wembley in November, 1957, but it was enough for him to come to the opinion: "Duncan was unique. When I played with him for England, he was just a kid really, but he was a terrific player, going through midfield like a battleship. As well as being strong, tough and quick, he was a great header of the ball, two-footed and liked to tackle. He could hit the diagonal passes and had a strong shot. He would be worth a fortune in today's game."

John Doherty, one of the Busby Babes whose early promise was cut short by injury and a transfer to Leicester City, was a team-mate who says: "It was always obvious that Duncan Edwards was going to be an exceptional player. Duncan was a big, strong lad with good feet, he was powerful in the air and it was difficult to pinpoint a weakness in his game. You would have to say he was magnificent, and consistently so.

"He was so fit and possessed such an incredible appetite for the game. More than anything else, he wanted to play. He barely suffered an injury before Munich, God bless him, and it makes me think, when I might be feeling sorry for myself, that I'm sure Duncan would have liked to have had an injury like me and lived. It could be said that he paid dearly for his love affair with the game. I saw him as a future captain of United and England. He had the stature; he was a commanding person with a presence about him and a certain arrogance in his game. Probably it is impossible to be a great player without a touch of arrogance, although arrogance played no part in his personality when he was not on the pitch."

Indeed, everyone who knew Duncan Edwards speaks of his unassuming nature, his modesty, even his shyness, and the nice way he handled his early acclaim. It's clear that in addition to being blessed with exceptional physique and talent, he had the temperament and character to have sustained a remarkable career.

It was typical of him that after the fateful game in Belgrade he sent a thoughtful but poignant telegram to Mrs Dorman, his landlady in Gorse Avenue, Stretford, saying: "All flights cancelled flying tomorrow – Duncan."

Tragically they did fly. Seven of the players were killed along with three members of staff. Eight of the nine sports writers on board also perished and Duncan Edwards was left fighting desperately for his life suffering from massive injuries in the Rechts der Isar Hospital.

Harry Gregg, survivor and hero who went back into the wrecked plane despite the risk of an explosion to rescue a baby and her mother, says: "Jimmy Murphy asked Bill Foulkes and I to stay for a few days so that those lying in hospital wouldn't realise the full extent of the accident.

"Eventually Professor Maurer, chief surgeon at the hospital, took Jimmy, Bill and myself round the wards and would stop at the foot of each bed to tell us their chances of survival. The Boss: 50-50 because he was a strong man, Jackie Blanchflower OK, Duncan 50-50.

"Duncan woke up when we went into his room and he asked us: 'What time is kick-off?' Quick as a flash Jimmy Murphy told him: 'Three o' clock, son.' Duncan responded: 'Get stuck in.'

"Bill and Î came home and I remember about 10 days afterwards all the newspapers in my house kept disappearing. I couldn't figure what was going on until I realised they were being hidden from me. Big Duncan had died. I found that hard.

It hit me terribly. Yes, that was Munich."

Duncan Edwards fought bravely in hospital for his life for 15 days. Frank Taylor of the *News Chronicle*, the only surviving journalist, said it was only Duncan's stupendous spirit that had kept him battling for as long as he did.

One of the doctors at the Rechts der Isar Hospital said afterwards: "I have seen death many, many times, but not like this. In all my years I have never seen a hospital staff so upset. This boy we have never seen before, he comes to our hospital – but he is so young, so strong, and so brave. Ach, but he had no chance."

As Frank Taylor wrote: "There were many tears that day in Munich, and far beyond, for a boy who had taken the world of sport by storm; who epitomized the power and zest and all that's best in British sport. A worthy young sports idol for the youth of the nation. Duncan Edwards was unforgettable. So long, Dunc. It was great while it lasted."

My colleague on the *Manchester Evening News*, Doug Slight, who had been reporting from Munich, wrote:

"Team-mates of Manchester United's plucky young footballer Duncan Edwards wept in the Rechts der Isar Hospital here today when they were told that football's wonder boy had lost his 15-day fight for life. The lion-hearted Edwards died peacefully in his sleep, with no pain, at 2.15am today, after a desperate last-minute battle to save him. About midnight doctors noticed that his circulation was failing. Injections caused a temporary improvement but his strength ebbed away. Nurses at his bedside, well used to suffering and sudden death, broke down and wept as the flame of life for which they had fought so hard flickered out."

Duncan's parents, Sarah and Gladstone Edwards, his fiancée Molly Leach and his friend Jimmy Payne, flew out to Munich and Duncan's body was flown home on Saturday, February 22. He was buried four days later at Dudley Cemetery not far from where he grew up.

A larger than life bronze statue now stands in the market place in his hometown of Dudley, and in the nearby St. Francis Church there are two stained-glass windows, unveiled by Sir Matt Busby in 1961, dedicated to his lasting memory.

As Sir Matt summed up at the ceremony: "I unveil these windows on behalf of Manchester United, in memory of this truly amazing boy who, apart from being a great footballer, devoted his life to sport and all the worthwhile things in life. These windows should keep alive his name forever, and they will shine always as monuments and examples to the youth of Dudley and the youth of England."

DUNCAN EDWARDS - CAREER STATS

BORN:	Dudley, Worcestershire
DATE OF BIRTH:	October 1 1936
JOINED UNITED:	June 1952
UNITED LEAGUE APPS:	151
GOALS:	20
INT. CAPS (England):	18
GOALS:	5

1953-1973

Sir Bobby Charlton

If ever a man was in love with football it has got to be Sir Bobby Charlton, former player now a director, who, despite all his success, still has a passion and enthusiasm for Manchester United that has shone through his life for well over half a century.

Football has been good to him of course and made him probably one of the most celebrated and recognised footballers on the planet. Way back at the height of the Cold War I remember travelling with United through Berlin and getting a hard time from the East German border guards at Checkpoint Charlie. It hadn't helped when one of our party had signed the inevitable form as 'James Bond' and the grim-faced soldiers were not amused – until they spotted Bobby Charlton on the bus and suddenly everyone was smiling again and asking for his autograph!

From Ashington to Azerbaijan his name is known and for all the right reasons. For here is a footballer who not only had an astonishing natural talent, but who graced the game because he played it the right way.

Bobby Charlton represents everything that is good about football, but what truly amazes me is how his commitment to Manchester United is as fierce as a director of his beloved club as it was when he was a thrusting Busby Babe setting out on his career over 50 years ago.

In fact he astonished me when I talked to him recently and he told me that the happiest moment in his football life came when Sir Alex Ferguson's team completed the unique treble by winning the European Champions League in 1999.

I said I found it difficult to believe that a man who had actually played in a European Cup-winning team and who also won a World Cup playing for England could say he got more satisfaction from watching as a spectator.

I had clearly underestimated what Manchester United means to him as he replied: "I have got to say that the best moment of my life, outside my family of course, was when Manchester United became European champions to crown their treble season. How can I say that after actually playing and winning in a European final? The answer is that I was able to relax and savour it more when I was just a spectator.

"In '68 there was this feeling that we simply had to win. The significance after Munich and the pressure took the pleasure out of it. It was not an easy match to play in. On the other hand in Barcelona I have never felt so happy in football terms in my life. Barcelona was made for us!

"It was pure Manchester United. We had hardly been in the Bayern Munich box and then suddenly Peter Schmeichel goes up and we get two goals in the last few minutes. Oh the drama of it! I think I jumped two rows of UEFA and FIFA people in front of where I was sitting.

"Time stood still for me until I did what all players do with those kinds of goals and that is to look along the line to make sure there's no offside flag going up. I was relieved to find that Bayern had a player on each post so both goals were good. They perhaps made a mistake there.

"Anyway, it was a fantastic result and Sir Alex Ferguson had the players to make it happen. Hopefully, because he always has good players, it will happen again too."

So no dreamer living on past glories here, more a

latter-day fan for whom the odyssey of Manchester United is far from at an end. He talks even more excitedly about the present-day United than he does about his own exploits and he has tremendous faith in Sir Alex Ferguson. Indeed, Bobby was one of the directors who pushed hardest for Alex Ferguson to take over from Ron Atkinson as manager in 1986. His faith has never wavered either.

"When people were talking about it being time for him to go I never lost any sleep," he told me. "I never thought he was going to go. I think he is desperate for another Champions League, but he's also desperate for another Premiership title and another FA Cup."

It was Sir Bobby who described Old Trafford as a theatre of dreams and it is clearly an ongoing dream for one of United's most distinguished sons.

No wonder Matt Busby in later years looked back on the dire days of the Munich air crash and said: "When things looked their blackest after the accident, and there were times when I felt great despair, I was enormously cheered to think that Bobby Charlton was there. His presence was a great source of inspiration to keep working for the restoration of Manchester United."

The football life and times of Bobby Charlton is inextricably woven into the history of Manchester United because he is the thread that more than anyone else stitches together the story that runs from the time Sir Matt Busby woke a sleeping giant to introduce his bubbling Busby Babes of the Fifties to the daring deeds and achievements of Sir Alex Ferguson's teams.

European football with its triumphs and tragedy has certainly shaped Bobby's career as he explains: "The first time I noticed European football was when we got a television set at home and I saw Real Madrid beat Rheims 4-3 in the first-ever final in 1956.

"Manchester United were not in the European Cup in that

first season but we were there the following year and what a sensational start in the opening round. We beat Anderlecht 2-0 in Belgium and then in the second leg in Manchester - played at Maine Road because we didn't have floodlights at Old Trafford – we won by an incredible 10-0.

"I was away doing my National Service in the Army at that time but I saw the match. The Company Sergeant Major at my unit near Shrewsbury drove me to the game and we watched from the stand. Even the floodlights were a novelty and everyone got very excited. They were entitled to as well because Anderlecht were a top side with Belgian internationals.

"It was all so new to us of course, so much so that some of the lads were taking tins of food and kettles to the away games because the rumour went round that we wouldn't get looked after very well.

"It was nonsense of course but it was certainly a huge step into the unknown. We just didn't know what to expect, but it was all so exciting. It was such a change from League football and the public got right behind the European scene. That Lowry painting showing all those matchstick people 'Going to the Match' captured the expectation and summed it all up.

"After Anderlecht we beat Borussia Dortmund and Athletic Bilbao. Then we came up against Real Madrid and lost the first leg of our semi-final 3-1. They kept hitting us on the break and we weren't used to that.

"I got into the team for the second leg against Real which we drew 2-2. I scored but couldn't believe the pace of it. I have always fancied the stamina of English teams and we were fit. We were never out of it but Real were unbelievable

"It was all such a great adventure, more so perhaps because Manchester United had had to go against the wishes of the football authorities in England to take part.

"Sir Matt Busby, who was a very progressive person, believed that it was right for Manchester United, when we started winning championships, to be in Europe playing against the best. He had a lot of really good, gifted young players at the beginning of our careers. We had been playing really well, and even though we had lost in the semi-finals against Real Madrid in our first season in the European Cup we thought we were capable of winning it the following year.

"But midway through the season came the dreadful accident at Munich, a great tragedy for the club, for the city of Manchester and, I suppose, for the whole country. It was especially tragic to lose a team just at the time when it was going to break into the elite and have world exposure. We were ready for it. We were right and we were starting to learn about European ways of playing.

"Sir Matt was a great visionary and he had developed a youth system that was not usual in Europe. The dropping of experienced players to make way for youngsters was bold but it paid off. I feel United had stolen a march on the rest of football and had come up with something very special.

"I was just one of many talented youngsters coming through at the time. But the accident happened and Sir Matt Busby, in his wisdom, said we had to go on and that we would need five years to get over the tragedy and to, maybe, have a team that was comparable.

"I thought it was unlikely that we'd get a team good enough to do well in Europe, but we won the FA Cup five years, almost to the day, after he said that's how long it would take. Then we won the League and qualified for the European Cup in 1965. We lost the semi-final against Partizan in Belgrade, which seemed like a great tragedy at the time, but we won the Championship again to qualify for another bid in Europe, and we managed to go right through to the final in 1968.

"One of the great matches I was privileged to play in – maybe the greatest - was so dramatic and took so much out of me. It was the semi-final against Real Madrid. We were 1-0 ahead from the first leg, but at half-time in Madrid we were 3-1 down. In the dressing room we didn't know what to say. We were so demoralised. All the dreams about putting it right after Munich…well, they would have to wait and maybe we wouldn't be able to get that far again for a long time.

"In the second half, though, we lifted our game, marked tighter and fought harder. We kept going and kept going and then David Sadler got a goal. Not a great goal but it was a goal that put us level on aggregate. Then George Best picked the ball up on the right side of the field. I was behind the play and I can remember seeing a red shirt way ahead of me and thinking: 'A red shirt; that's good'. Then I realised it wasn't a forward. It was our centre-half who never scored goals at all. Bill Foulkes had pushed forward because we were desperate to win and he just stroked the ball past the goalkeeper inside the far post. Suddenly we were winning. We couldn't believe it. It was so emotional and we had so many fans in Madrid on a really hot, humid night. Unbelievably we had qualified for the final – and the final was to be played at Wembley Stadium against Benfica.

"They were one of the great teams with marvellous players – not just Eusébio but other really great players. We were playing at home and the whole country wanted us to win. It was very important. We had to win the European Cup. It was the thing that had to be done at this club. I scored a goal early in the second half but then they equalised. A disaster. I remember Eusébio breaking through with a few minutes to go and when he shot at goal, my whole world was about to collapse. But Alex Stepney held it. He didn't just block it - he held it. I couldn't believe it. Then the final whistle went and we had another half-hour to play. We were used to playing extra-time but I think it was a bit foreign to Europeans. They didn't like the extra half-hour. Within five or six minutes we scored three goals. It was unbelievable. You couldn't see the crowd because the game was played under floodlights. But you could certainly hear them.

"When the final whistle went everyone charged after Matt Busby. It was just magic. I will never, ever forget it. Everybody said it was something for the players who weren't there. It was an enormous boost for the club and, of course, it was seen all around the world on TV. I suppose that is one of the stories that created the legend which is Manchester United."

United's European journey didn't stop with the success of 1968, of course. Europe is an ongoing challenge and Bobby has stayed with it, trying not to look back too much because that could be a negative approach and he is still always looking to the next match. "I get just as excited and I love Champions League games, even if I do worry to death about them," he says.

At the height of his powers, there was no sight more majestic than Bobby Charlton running in full stride, cheeks puffed out with the effort, and unleashing one of his thunderous shots.

When he was in full flow for goal, there was a grace and beauty about him, a balletic quality, which singled him out as a player beautifully balanced who was so often like poetry in motion.

What also made him special was that he had a sporting spirit which saw him commit only one disciplinary offence in the whole of his career, and that a booking for failing to retreat at a free kick which was subsequently wiped off his record by the Football Association as a mistake! He was an idol without feet of clay, a gentleman and a sportsman supreme whose behaviour was exemplary both on and off the field.

He retired from football in 1973 and 11 years later he was elected a director of the club, a position he still holds along with many other appointments as a football consultant and sporting ambassador for Manchester United.

He was probably the first player to establish a coaching school and it ran for many years, with Londoner David Beckham one of his early pupils in Manchester.

He has held sponsored coaching clinics the length and breadth of the country as well as in countries like South Africa, but more and more he works in his capacity as a United director as an ambassador on behalf of the club.

Says Bobby: "My first business venture came when one of my friends, Freddie Pye, asked me to come onto the board of a little travel company in Hale called Halba Travel. Then after I had done some coaching with kids in Argentina I thought I could do that at home and with Ray Whelan, a staff coach, we started the Bobby Charlton Soccer Schools. We tried to make it fun and had an unbelievable response. It expanded all over the world and it's nice to think the FA followed us by introducing their own fun camps. Now I enjoy old players, like David Beckham and Paul Merson, coming up to me and saying that when they were kids they had been to one of my schools.

Nowadays I'm the director of an electrical company but mostly I work for Manchester United, not just as a director, but employed to represent them on various commercial enterprises all over the world. I seem to be travelling more and more but I enjoy everything about Manchester United and it's a labour of love."

It was always likely that Bobby Charlton would become a soccer player, given that his mother, Cissie, came from the famous Milburn soccer family in the North East of England. Three of her brothers, Jack, Jim and George, played for Leeds United, while a fourth brother, Stan, played for Leicester City. Cissie's cousin was the legendary Newcastle United centre-forward, 'Wor' Jackie Milburn, while grandfather 'Tanner' Milburn kept goal for his local team.

It was hardly surprising then that first Bobby's brother, Jack, grew up to play for Leeds United and England while Bobby himself soon attracted attention as a schoolboy and went on to enjoy an even more famous career. Born in Northumberland, the son of a miner in the coal pit village of Ashington, Bobby went to the local junior school where his team's first football shorts were run up by one of the lady teachers from wartime blackout curtaining.

Manchester United heard about him and on February 9, 1953, sent their chief scout, Joe Armstrong, to watch him in a game. Joe came dashing back to announce: "I had to peer through a mist, but what I saw was enough. This boy is going to be a world beater."

Later when he had begun to score goals for the England schoolboy team, scouts from all over came with offers to sign him. At one stage there were said to be as many as 18 clubs interested but he remembered his first promise to Joe Armstrong and came to Manchester United.

He first caught the eye of United fans playing in three successive FA Youth Cup-winning teams, starting in season 1953-54 by beating Wolves in the final. He became a regular reserve, scoring regularly and he must have wondered when he was going to get a chance in the first team, so flush with talent were United as the Busby Babes arrived on the scene. The call finally came for a debut against Charlton Athletic at Old Trafford on October 6, 1956, and Bobby took a gamble. "Mr Busby asked me if I was OK. Actually I had a sprained ankle but I wasn't going to admit to it and I crossed my fingers and said yes," he explained. It was worth the gamble as he scored twice in a 4-2 win, though he was dropped for the following match at Sunderland one week later to make way for the return of the injured Tommy Taylor.

Competition was severe and at first Bobby played only when there was an injury to Taylor, Dennis Viollet or Billy Whelan in the forward line. Gradually, though, his appearances became more regular and towards the end of the 1956-57 season he had settled into the side on a fairly regular basis. His eye for goal was remarkable and though surrounded by more experienced players, he made his presence felt to score 10 goals from 14 appearances to help clinch the first Championship success of the newly-emerging Babes.

Bobby also won a place in the FA Cup team for the latter stages of the 1956-57 season, scoring in the semi-final win against Birmingham City and then playing in the final against Aston Villa when they seemed set to achieve a League and Cup Double until goalkeeper Ray Wood had his cheekbone smashed in a collision with Peter McParland.

Still only 18, he also made his debut in the European Cup that season with a prominent display for such a young player in the 2-2 semi-final, second leg against Real Madrid on April 25. It was a vintage era and it needed a special talent to break into a side which seemed to score goals for fun and indeed had rattled in 103 on their way to winning the League.

It meant he still had to fight for a permanent place and it didn't really come until midway through the following season of 1957-58. When he got in, though, he really made his mark, such as a hat-trick in a 7-2 home win over Bolton on January 18 and scoring both goals in an FA Cup fourth-round tie, won 2-0 at Old Trafford against Ipswich the following week.

He also took to Europe in an effortless stride when he was called up to play in the first leg of the quarter-final against Red Star Belgrade at Old Trafford. He scored in a 2-1 win to book a trip for the fateful second leg in Belgrade. He scored twice in the 3-3 draw which secured United a place in the semi-finals and, like the rest of the young men flying home the following day for Saturday's match against Wolves, the football world lay at his feet.

But then of course came the heart-breaking tragedy of the crash as their plane made a third attempt to take off after landing at Munich to refuel on the journey home. It was just after three o'clock on Thursday afternoon, the 6th of February 1958, a date etched grimly into the history of football. Of the 44 people on board, 23 died in the crash or shortly afterwards.

Eight of them were players. Nine survived but two never played again because of their injuries. Bobby Charlton was knocked out and was dragged clear of the wreckage by team-mate Harry Gregg. He was kept in hospital suffering from concussion, shock and cuts, but he was relatively fortunate.

Bobby was sent home to rest on his return to England but returned to action for the FA Cup sixth round against West Bromwich Albion on March 1, and to help the poignantly patched-up team go all the way to the final at Wembley in May where they lost to Bolton.

Then began the long and difficult process of rebuilding. Players came and went but Charlton was a constant. Indeed, many felt that he had gone out to Belgrade a boy but after the experience of Munich quickly became a man.

He was a foundation for the recovery, as Busby freely acknowledged.

He certainly threw himself into playing for his club again and in the season after Munich, 1958-59, he played 38 League games and scored 28 goals. He played mostly on the left wing at this time, a position he didn't particularly like because from his point of view he didn't feel involved enough in the play. He was still on the wing in the team that beat Leicester to win the FA Cup in 1963, although given the freedom to rove around the field and get into shooting range.

By the 1964-65 season Matt Busby had moved him into a midfield position wearing the No 8 shirt. He became a much more influential player and his skills as a creative player as well as a marksman were given more reign. He was a key figure in the Championship success of that season. His scoring dropped to 10 goals, but his passing pulled defences apart as well as his ability to ghost past opponents with an ease, a grace and an acceleration that were lovely to watch.

It was at this stage that his international career reached a peak. He had made his England debut just a few months after the Munich accident, playing against Scotland at Hampden, and over the next 12 years he won 106 caps while scoring 49 goals, a scoring record which still stands. His great year came in 1966 when two typical Charlton goals against Portugal, fierce shots that gave the goalkeeper no chance, put England through to the final of the World Cup.

Charlton was a tireless and inspiring player at Wembley in the final against West Germany. His relentless foraging, telling passes and scoring threat caused problems throughout the match and made sure that the German half-back, Franz Beckenbauer, had little time to prompt his own forwards. Normal time finished level at 1-1 and then in extra time the fluency of Charlton went a long way towards helping Geoff Hurst score his famous record World Cup final hat-trick for a 4-2 victory. Bobby, who confirmed his world-class ranking, shared the pitch with his brother Jack. The climax was tearful but Bobby wouldn't be ashamed of that.

Soon after the 1966 international triumph he was voted Footballer of the Year by England's soccer writers, an honour quickly followed by European Footballer of the Year, as well as an award from the referees as a Model Player.

Bobby Charlton was not finished with honours yet, though. He was in his pomp now and was one of the outstanding players along with Denis Law, David Herd, George Best, Nobby Stiles and Alex Stepney who won the Championship of 1966-67. He was a League ever-present and scored 12 goals from midfield to qualify for another crack at Europe. This was the peak of his career as United swept to their great European Cup triumph of 1968. Bobby felt it was the club's destiny to become Champions of Europe that season, exactly 10 years after Munich.

"My thoughts on the day of the final against Benfica were that we had come too far and been through too much for us to fail in that final game," he declared.

Bobby scored with a rare header for 1-1 at the end of normal time and then added the last goal in a 4-1 victory. He was so drained afterwards that he missed the celebration banquet and stayed in his room.

In all he played First Division football for 17 seasons to total a club record of 604 appearances, plus two as a sub, and score a record 199 goals. When he retired, his last game was typically an obscure fixture against Verona in Italy in the Anglo-Italian tournament at the end of season 1972-73. He still managed to score twice in a 4-1 win, however!

He was elected a director of United in 1984. He was knighted in the birthday honours of 1994 after being awarded an OBE and CBE in the course of a distinguished career which also saw him make a brief foray into management at Preston, as well as later becoming a director of Wigan at the invitation of his pal Freddie Pye.

Bobby Charlton always insisted that it would be the matches and medals he would want to talk about in later life to his children and friends, not the money, and he has remained in love with the game.

He admits he has been fortunate with injuries: "I never had anything serious. I still have all my cartilages and I didn't know what a hamstring injury was. Perhaps it was just luck, though I always had a bit of beef on me and it was often the thin ones with no protection who got hurt. David Beckham is what I would say, well put together, and he doesn't miss many games either. And I never wore pads, which you didn't have to in my day.

"The longest I was out with injury was two or three weeks, except for a hernia, but that wasn't a football injury, I did that playing golf! I remember reporting back for pre-season training and telling Ted Dalton our physio that I had this lump. He examined me and said that's you out for three months, you need a hernia operation. It had been a baking hot summer and the courses were rock hard. I had caught the golf bug and I think I just played too much. I don't think the boss was best pleased!"

Now turned 70 he is still very fit and in 1997 he marked his 60th birthday by accepting an invitation to play in a match between a Salford Select XI and Moss Side Amateur Reserves. The only condition he made was that he should be allowed to play the full 90 minutes without being substituted. Playing a bit part is not Bobby Charlton's idea of football, even at near pension age!

"It was my birthday present to myself," he declared, and one suspects that it was his favourite gift!

It's really a matter, though, of what he has given to us, as the late Geoffrey Green of The Times timelessly expressed it in his book: "It was the explosive facets of his play that will remain fresh in memory. His thinning fair hair streaming in the wind, he moved like a ship in full sail. He always possessed an elemental quality, jinking, changing feet and direction, turning gracefully on the ball, or accelerating through a gap surrendered by a confused enemy, he could be gone like the wind."

But as I have tried to portray in this tribute there is much more to Bobby Charlton than his playing ability. As Sir Matt Busby once put it to me: "The name of Bobby Charlton will stand forever. Time will add to his stature rather than diminish it. He arrived at Old Trafford a shy, perhaps slightly bewildered boy of 15. The shy boy has blossomed now into a man with a great sense of assurance, confidence and responsibility. His heart and mind have been forever at Old Trafford, wrapped up in the interests of Manchester United. We trod the same road for a great part of our careers, aiming for the same achievements and sharing the disappointments as well as the triumphs.

"One of the delightful aspects of his character is that he has retained a tremendous enthusiasm. Losing always meant something to him as well as winning. It made him a better professional.

"His shyness never showed on the field of play. I remember the goals he scored when he was only 18. I have vividly implanted on my mind the sight of him volleying David Pegg's centre home in the FA Cup semi-final against Birmingham at Hillsborough in the year before Munich. It was a tremendously-hit shot and he repeated it in his first international playing for England against Scotland at Hamden Park.

"I can't begin to list all the other wonderful goals he has scored or list his proud international career, except to say what a marvellous contribution he made in the World Cup of 1966 with his so valuable goals. Could I also ever forget his header in the final of the European Cup in 1968, a goal that set us on the path towards the victory that had been our aim for so long?

"He has broken all records and won everything possible there is to win. Yet he has remained completely unspoiled, still prepared to do more than his fair share for Manchester United."

Tributes are legion, like this from his old England manager, the late Sir Alf Ramsey: "Probably the best known footballer in the world, he has been a wonderful ambassador for England, not only as a footballer, but also in the way in which he has upheld the prestige of his country in every possible sense."

Opponents admired him just as warmly, like his old foe of Benfica and Portugal, Eusébio, who despite defeat said about him after the European Cup final: "My good friend Bobby Charlton even scored with his head following a corner from George Best. As a sportsman I congratulated him because he had never scored in that way. He is a great man, a great football man and a great friend. In the world of football, friendship is very important even though we defend different clubs and countries. He is a true gentleman and my friendship with Bobby Charlton is very strong."

Jimmy Murphy, his mentor when he first arrived at Old Trafford, used to play in practice matches with his young charges and Bobby couldn't understand when his boss used to come up behind him and kick the back of his legs.

"I used to wonder what on earth was going on. Now when I look back I realise he was trying to toughen me up to take the knocks, and perhaps to encourage me to pass the ball a bit quicker!"

Bobby would be the first to admit that Murphy and the other coaches like Bert Whalley worked hard to polish the diamond that had arrived from the North East.

Jimmy recalls: "Bobby was a difficult pupil. He did so many things superbly and by instinct, but he kept spoiling it by hitting long balls to the right or left wing and then standing still. It was beautiful to watch, and yet so many of the long passes were made when a shorter one would have been better. To his eternal credit Bobby never shirked these training sessions.

"He was seen through the mists of Northumberland one day by chief scout Joe Armstrong as a boy with a golden future. How right he was, for Bobby Charlton became everyone's ideal of a soccer player and a sportsman."

I guess it was his enthusiasm and appetite for the game that saw him come through the Murphy mangle and take the lessons to heart.

And his fondness for football is just as much in evidence now all these years later, as I was reminded when I interviewed him for an article in last year's Carling Cup final programme when Manchester United beat Wigan 4-0. His thoughts on the state of today's football came bubbling out.

"So much about football is better today, the pitches, the ball, security for the players, medical support, nutrition. Nothing is missed if they think it will improve the players or the team. We were very basic in my day, but don't run away with the idea that we wouldn't be able to play in today's game. With all the advantages available now we would simply be better players," he said.

"Big money doesn't help make better players, in fact I believe a hungry sportsman is likely to be more dangerous than a comfortable one and is perhaps willing to go that little bit further. So it becomes more important than ever to get players with the right character who want to play because it's a love of playing and winning that drives them.

"I think more football clubs should take former players on to their boards. I think we can be a bridge between the playing staff and the directors. I can't teach Alex Ferguson anything about managing, none of us can, but occasionally he comes for a chat. I might tell him something. It's probably in one ear and out the other, but he is very gracious about it. He expects my support and I am happy to give it."

And that's Sir Bobby Charlton, half a century down the line, proud of his achievements but as enthusiastic about football and Manchester United as he was all those years ago when he was first spotted ghosting through that Northumberland mist.

SIR BOBBY CHARLTON - CAREER STATS

BORN:	Ashington, Northumberland
DATE OF BIRTH:	October 11 1937
JOINED UNITED:	June 1953
UNITED LEAGUE APPS:	606
GOALS:	199
INT. CAPS (England):	106
GOALS:	49

1957-1971

Nobby Stiles

In his long and distinguished career, Sir Bobby Charlton has played with or against some of the finest footballers in the world. So it came as perhaps something of a surprise to hear the former Manchester United and England captain describe Nobby Stiles as "my favourite footballer."

They are pals of course, and the pair of them are the only two Englishmen to hold winners medals from both the World Cup and European Cup.

They have been through a lot together, too, but even so, there was no disguising the heartfelt tribute and admiration as Sir Bobby went on to explain: "As a midfield player with United I used to turn round and see Nobby behind me and think: 'We're OK.'

"It was the same playing for England, particularly if the opposition had someone a bit hard playing for them. I was always glad Nobby was on our side."

Sir Bobby made his remarks speaking at a dinner thrown by publishers Hodder and Stoughton to launch Nobby'sautobiography, *Nobby Stiles After the Ball*, and it was an indication of his standing in the game that also there in support were two more of their 1966 World Cup-winning team-mates, Sir Geoff Hurst and George Cohen.

Nobby Stiles is in fact probably not just Bobby Charlton's favourite footballer but the nation's, certainly among those who witnessed his toothless and joyful jig around Wembley after England had beaten West Germany in the final of the World Cup in 1966.

But for all his success and reaching the pinnacle with those two priceless medals, it has not left Nobby – or Norbert to give him his Sunday-best name – a wealthy man, nor has life been easy for this son of an undertaker raised in modest circumstances in downtown Collyhurst, a footballing hothouse producing many fine players, but a far cry from the Cheshire villages that are home to today's stars of Manchester United.

He had a happy childhood, and as the book makes clear he had loving parents, but in many respects his whole life was a battle. You might say it is for any erstwhile footballer striving to make the grade in a career as competitive as professional football, but in Nobby's case there were several additional hurdles to surmount.

Being born during the war in a cellar, while an air raid took place on Manchester seemed an omen for a toddler who not long after would be knocked down by a bus. He recovered from that, but more serious for an ambitious sportsman was poor eyesight, shades of Denis Law here, a problem which Nobby says came to a head in a match against Everton at Goodison Park.

"I went to receive a throw-in from the wing-half and I suddenly realised I was guessing when it came to timing the ball and to where and to whom I was going to play it. I was given a man to mark and in the flow of play I frequently lost sight of him. It was a terrible shock but, perhaps out of fear of what I would be told if I raised the issue with Matt Busby and was sent to see specialist, I kept quiet."

It was Harry Gregg who came to his rescue after noting his struggle to see properly when they were playing cards, of all things. He went to see Busby and said: "You know, boss, you just have to do something about Nobby's eyesight. The kid is really struggling. He's putting down the wrong cards. He just can't read them. We just have to imagine how it's affecting his play."

And it did affect his football with some spectacularly clumsy tackles that Bobby Charlton sympathetically insisted were simply mistimed efforts that were down to poor eyesight. "He didn't tackle people so much as just bump into them," he said.

At the same time it wasn't just footballers who were at risk when Nobby was about. He frequently left an accidental trail of destruction behind him. I remember the splendidly furnished hotel we stayed in near Windsor in preparation for the 1968 European Cup final at Wembley. Nobby looked admiringly at the sturdy oak panelling and huge wood mantelpiece and said how much he admired its solid look, slapping one particular carved piece which promptly came away in his hand.

His eyesight was such that his team-mates swear that at one after-match banquet Nobby left the room and was missing for ages because he had blindly wandered into the wrong room on his way back from the 'Gents.' They say he only realised that he had sat down among strangers when he spotted this girl wearing a long white dress and it dawned on him that he was at a wedding reception.

The club finally sorted him out and so began the trademark big black specs and later the ritual of contact lenses for training and playing. It brought a marked improvement in his football, though his new-look didn't evidently impress England colleague Jack Charlton.

The pair met up when they were chosen in a team representing the Football League against the Scottish League at Newcastle. Nobby says: "It was in the dressing room before the game that I first met Jack Charlton. We eyed each other across the room and I was not thrilled when he later recalled to the world his first impression of me. He said he saw this 'little Japanese-looking bastard fitting these bloody great things into his eyes.'"

Even with contact lenses Nobby was still a hard-tackling aggressive player, so much so that Jack Wood of the *Daily Mail* once suggested in a match report that he had put himself about to such telling effect that it looked as if he was trying to drum up trade for the family funeral business. His father was not best pleased.

Nobby was a Red from birth. "You didn't have much choice, it was all red where we lived in Collyhurst. My first recollection was the 1948 FA Cup final at the age of six. I used to go to Old Trafford as a kid. I'd stand on the Stretford End and also on the Warwick Road End above the tunnel. I used to dream that one day my name would be announced over the tannoy: 'Number four, Norbert Stiles.'"

While he watched the Busby Babes take the game by storm, his own career was progressing well. "I started playing for St. Patrick's School aged 10, and by the time I was 11 I was playing for the two teams above me. I was noticed playing for Manchester boys where I was captain and selected for England schoolboys."

Nobby won five caps for England and joined United as a schoolboy at the age of 15 in 1957. A year later he was in the youth team and says: "I can remember playing Newcastle away and beating them 8-1. We had a very strong side, but then Munich happened. Munich had an unbelievable impact on the club. We had been training that afternoon when we were told to go home early because the plane had crashed. I boarded the bus back to Piccadilly where I bought the *Evening Chronicle*. There were photographs of the people who had died. I got the bus to Collyhurst and went into church and just cried for an hour. They were my idols.

"Duncan Edwards is still the greatest player I have ever seen. He had everything. He could strike a ball with both feet, he was a great header of the ball and could drop his shoulder like Bobby

Charlton. If United were losing he could play centre-forward. If we were under the cosh he could play at centre-half. In 1966 Duncan Edwards would have been 29. He died at a criminally young age.

"My idol from that team though was little Eddie Colman, snake hips, from Salford. He didn't know it but I used to clean his boots special and make sure they were spotless. I was nothing like him as a player but I tried to model myself on him. I know it sounds terrible but my career must have been helped by that tragedy. I mean, how could I have displaced anyone like Eddie Colman? He was a genius.

"After Munich, a lot of players got pushed into the first team too soon but Jimmy Murphy, Busby's right-hand man, kept me down in the youth team and I was grateful for that," he said.

Nobby made his first-team debut aged 18 in October 1960, away to Bolton at Burnden Park, in a 1-1 draw. Still reeling from Munich, the average age of the United side that day was just 22 years, 116 days. Stiles stayed in the side for the rest of the season, making a total of 26 League appearances as the side finished 7th. It was a difficult apprenticeship for him as Matt Busby rebuilt with finishing positions of 15th and 19th, but he did share in the FA Cup run of 1963 that saw United beat Leicester City 3-1 at Wembley. Nobby made four appearances in the Cup run but missed out on the final as he battled with Maurice Setters for a regular place in the side.

Says Nobby: "The spirit in the club was unbelievable and so was the fact that we won the Cup just five years after losing so many great players. In the early Sixties I was in and out of the side and it wasn't until late '64 that I really became a regular."

In season 1964-65 he missed only one game on the way to winning the Championship and he had settled into a position in central defence alongside Bill Foulkes at centre-half. The half-back line of Crerand, Foulkes and Stiles prospered and with another League title in season 1966-67 he hardly missed a match. They had proved effective in Europe, too, reaching the semi-final of the European Cup in 1966

After knocking out Benfica United were favourites to go all the way but with George Best injured they were beaten in the semi-finals by Partizan Belgrade. Two years later they went all the way to become the first English club to win the European Cup. They did it the hard way, too, with their old foes, Real Madrid, standing in their way in the semi-final.

Nobby, who had watched his Busby Babe heroes come unstuck against the super Spanish side a decade earlier, says: "We beat Real 1-0 at Old Trafford but in the return leg in the Bernabeu, we were 3-1 down at half-time. Nobody remembered that on aggregate there was only one goal in the game and Matt didn't moan, he just said: 'Go out, attack them and enjoy it.' And we did. Bill Foulkes told me not to go forward and I wasn't going to argue with him. David Sadler scored, and then Bill Foulkes got an equaliser. Bill Foulkes of all people, the man who never left defence – and after telling me not to go forward too! I went to celebrate with him but he was having none of it and told me to get back in defence.

"In the final I was given the job of marking the great Eusébio. I tried to stick to him like glue but unfortunately, he lost me for a second and got a shot on goal. That shot could have prevented us from winning the European Cup but Alex Stepney pulled off a brilliant save and the rest is history."

It was the fourth time Stiles had been called upon to mark Eusébio, and just as he had done playing for England against Portugal he played him fairly with Eusébio denied a goal, bar a penalty he had taken and scored. Although Eusébio was always a threat Stiles came out on top. One newspaper reported that Eusébio had asked for more protection from the referee but Stiles doesn't believe he ever said it.

"I never went out to kick him. I respected him and found him all right," he says.

The final must have given Nobby a déjà vu feeling as the game reached the end of normal time with the score level. "For me it was the World Cup all over again when Germany pulled level just before the end. If the game had had another 10 minutes to go I think we would have lost. There we were, on top and in front, but when they equalised it knocked the heart out of us. We suddenly realised how tired we were," he explained.

But just as Nobby and his England team-mates had done, United pulled out something special in extra time to score three goals and win handsomely. The fact that Nobby Stiles was in both teams was, I'm sure, a key factor. His career and standing in the game was at a peak, but his bad-boy image still cast a long shadow, as he discovered when United played Estudiantes for the World Club Championship early the following season.

The first leg was played in Buenos Aires and as far as the Argentineans were concerned he was remembered for his part in the infamous World Cup game when Rattin had been sent off and Sir Alf Ramsey had referred to their team playing like 'animals'.

The hostility was evident from the moment the plane touched down. As the United players walked through the airport, an excitable commentator was announcing their arrival over the loudspeaker system.

"Bobby Charlton...El Supremo," he shouted. "George Best...El Beatle," he declared. Then his voice went up an octave and there was a great answering roar as he went on: "Nobby Stiles...El Bandido!"

That was just the start as Nobby discovered that the newspapers had reported the Estudiantes manager, Otto Gloria, saying that he was 'an assassin.' Estudiantes even ran an article in their match programme by the Benfica chief saying that he was 'brutal, badly intentioned and a bad sportsman.'

"I didn't expect the home fans to be on my side after that, but I think the referee must have read the programme, too, because

I didn't get much sympathy from him either," he said.

His particular problem was a wild young man called Carlos Bilardo who would surface a few years later as the manager who guided Argentina to their World Cup victory in Mexico in 1986. Not many players can claim to have been head-butted by a future national team manager, but that's what happened to Nobby Stiles when Bilardo was the Estudiantes hatchet man.

Says Stiles: "The butting was bad enough, but Bilardo then threw himself down as if it was me who had hit him. I think the referee was going to send me off, but I was able to point to the blood running from a cut eye and it made him change his mind.

"The stuff that was going in that game was unbelievable and you wouldn't get it nowadays because of the television cameras. I was sent off, not for a foul, but because I protested to the ref after a linesman had flagged me offside. I didn't think I was and I just threw my hands in the air. The referee sent me off for dissent. It was a bit silly and I was very upset because I thought I had let the side down. There was a lot going on and it seemed ridiculous that I should be sent off for waving my arms.

"Mind you, the referee was a funny chap. He was smoking a cigarette when we all came down the tunnel to go out on the pitch. A lot of people smoke but you don't expect to see the referee having a puff like that."

United lost 1-0 but that wasn't the end of his problems. He remembers coming out of the stadium after the match heading for the team bus. It was dark and shadowy when he suddenly felt something thrust into his back with a voice whispering into his ear: "Now then El Bandido." He thought his end had come, until he realised it was Brian Kidd.

Stiles missed the return leg in Manchester, suspended because of the dismissal. Estudiantes weren't as badly behaved in the Old Trafford leg, though there were two players sent off, Hugo Medina followed by George Best for retaliation. United went a goal down after five minutes, and even though Willie

Morgan scored near the end for 1-1 on the night, the match was lost on aggregate. Sir Matt Busby said afterwards: "The Argentinean Press crucified Nobby Stiles and it was quite disgraceful."

In many ways Nobby was a man of contrast, you loved him or you hated him. With his socks round his ankles and an ear-splitting grin revealing the absence of his front teeth, Nobby's World Cup jig of joy round Wembley Stadium danced him into the affections of fans because they knew they had just seen a footballer who had played his heart out for his country.

But there is no dodging his reputation as a hard man, and opposition fans, especially abroad, positively hated him. In addition to his trials and tribulations in Argentina he was hit on the head by a bottle thrown in Madrid, and hissed and spat at in Italy.

He is remembered for his exploits against the big teams like Real Madrid and Benfica in the European Cup, but Nobby's favourite European campaign came in the Inter-Cities Fairs Cup of 1964-65. It was a good season for the Reds, winning the League, but it was their run in Europe that he looks back on most fondly.

"We were at our peak and played some cracking football, scoring five or six goals in every round, sometimes even in the away legs. We opened cautiously enough with a 1-1 draw against Djurgardens in Sweden but demolished them 6-1 at Old Trafford with the help of a hat-trick from Denis Law. We went to Germany and won 6-1 against Borussia Dortmund, this time with a hat-trick from Bobby Charlton. We celebrated that one by winning 4-0 on our ground.

"It was tighter in the next round, understandably perhaps because we were up against Everton. It was 1-1 for us at home and then a 2-1 win at Goodison Park. We were back among the goals on our travels, though, beating Strasbourg 5-0 in France, which with a goalless second leg sent us into a semi-final against Ferencvaros feeling very confident.

"The only problem was that it had been a long, hard season because we also reached the semi-finals of the FA Cup involving a replay against Leeds United and fixture congestion meant it was June before we played the Hungarians. I know I had certainly been busy, playing 66 games if you include England U23 appearances. We won the first leg 3-2 at Old Trafford but lost 1-0 in Budapest.

"Away goals didn't count double in those days, so after losing the toss we had to go back to Budapest. By then it was June 16 and most footballers were on holiday! We lost 2-1 but we had won the Championship with a team bursting with goals. We had five players in double figures just for League goals. We were dripping with goals and I shall always remember that season for some great football. It was a very good team and great to be part of it."

While never the most elegant of performers, total commitment was the only way Nobby Stiles knew how to play, and coupled with his outstanding ability to read the game, he was a key member of United's defence throughout the successful Sixties.

Sir Matt Busby valued him enormously, and so did Sir Alf Ramsey who consistently selected him to knit together the more sophisticated thoroughbreds of his World Cup-winning team.

Ramsey played him just in front of his central defenders, Bobby Moore and Jack Charlton while Busby had him mostly alongside Bill Foulkes at centre-back. In both roles he was a ball winner and the provider of the simple pass, always showing an uncanny knack for spotting an attacking threat. Sir Bobby Charlton once told me that his pal reminded him of a sheepdog constantly rounding up those who strayed out of line and barking at them until they were back in the pen!

He made his debut for the full England side in 1965 after

being capped at schoolboy, youth and U23 level and he was a regular for two years to make a total of 28 appearances – scoring once!

He says: "Luckily we won the World Cup in those two years. The '66 World Cup wasn't about the 11 players who played at Wembley but the 22 players in the squad. Like Matt did at Old Trafford, Alf Ramsey created such a spirit amongst us all that if you kicked one of us, you kicked all of us."

Naturally his tendency to give his all, plus a bit more, in every match brought him controversy in the international arena. None more so than when he flattened Jacky Simon playing against France on the road to the final.

Nobby describes it: "I remember the tackle well enough. It was the one from hell, which is exactly where it threatened to put me. As I recall the build-up, we were attacking along the right with George Cohen on the ball and Simon, a very good player, tracking him. When the French goalkeeper, Marcel Aubour, gathered up the ball and threw it out to his team-mate, I was already on the move, watching the ball looping down and lining up my tackle.

"Maybe I should say what was in my mind as I went into the tackle that would create such a storm of headlines and criticism. It was to hit the ball - and him - just as he turned. It is not a foul if you go through the ball, hitting it with all the force you have, and that takes you through the player. That is a hard but legal tackle, and that was my ambition. The objective is not to hurt the player but to remind him of the force of body contact in the game, to announce your presence so that the next time you are in his vicinity, he will think twice about doing something fancy, and possibly dangerous, with the ball.

"What went wrong was that while I was following an old instruction of Matt Busby's, who always used to say, 'Norrie, let him know you are there in the first five minutes,' the ball had gone. Simon, the playmaker, who liked to stroke it around, had on this occasion whipped the ball away at first contact. That compounded my mistiming, making the tackle look even more horribly late. The crowd shrieked, and although the referee, Arturo Yamaski, a Peruvian, took no action, a FIFA observer in the stand did. He booked me and took me within an inch of being banished from the World Cup."

The Football Association wanted him out of the team for the next game against Argentina, already a powder-keg clash, but Alf Ramsey stood by his man and told the FA that if Nobby went, so did he!

As Nobby puts it: "When I was being hung, drawn and quartered by the Press, the television panellists and the high-ups in the Football Association, and the world ruling body FIFA wanted me thrown out of the tournament, that was when Alf stood up for me against a world that suddenly seemed very hostile indeed, and when I became indebted to him for the rest of my life."

Nobby is always eager to express his appreciation of the help he has received along the way, and like many of the Busby Babes and the team of the Sixties, he doesn't hesitate also to acknowledge the debt he owes to Jimmy Murphy, Sir Matt Busby's right-hand man who coached and cajoled the youngsters on the their way through the junior ranks.

"I have Jimmy to thank for making me into the player I became," he says. "He was the main reason why from the 1940s through to the 1960s Manchester United produced so many world-class players who later became legends. He was a tireless worker, out on the training field morning, noon and night. Next to his family, his only other interest and love was Manchester United," he explained.

Jimmy made an immediate impact on the youthful recruit from Collyhurst and on his first day at Old Trafford told him: "This, son," he said with his arm round his shoulder and full of enthusiasm and bulldog tenacity, "is the greatest club in the whole world and when you pull on that famous red jersey and run out of this tunnel on to that pitch you'll feel a special sensation in your whole body, there is no other thrill like it.

"You'll be happy here and we want you to enjoy it with all your heart and soul. Nobby, son, you'll never regret joining us – there is no other club in the world like us."

On another occasion after a hard training session he told a group of the newcomers: "This is the place to be, lads, you'll all get a chance here. Show me you can play and before you know it you will be playing in the first team."

As Nobby says: "We kids used to like hearing Jimmy saying things like that because it encouraged us. He was the heartbeat of the club, an unsung hero."

Jimmy always returned the admiration, possibly because he could see a reflection of himself as a tough-tackling half-back. Nobby needed his support, too, because when he first arrived at United he was so small and scrawny that many of the other young players looked at him in disbelief.

But Murphy simply told the other boys: "Don't worry about Nobby. He's a Collyhurst lad. They breed great boxers and footballers there. He can take care of himself."

Nobby Stiles played first-team football at Old Trafford for 11 seasons making a total of nearly 400 appearances in all competitions before suffering the effects of two cartilage operations, which brought his United career to an end at the age of 27.

Typically for a man of such spirit, he was far from calling it a day and he went, perhaps a little reluctantly, to Middlesbrough in 1971 for a transfer fee of £20,000. Such was his popularity, that unlike the hostile reception accorded to most players returning to their old clubs, there were welcoming banners for him when he arrived back with Middlesbrough to play against United, and he was given the warmest of welcomes.

After two seasons at Ayresome Park he moved for the same

fee to play for his good friend and former team-mate, Bobby Charlton, at Preston. Altogether he was at Deepdale for eight years, quitting as a player after a season to spend three years as a coach and then four as the manager.

Early on in his career he had married Kay, the sister of another United pal, Johnny Giles, and after finishing at Preston he joined his brother-in-law in Canada. John was manager of Vancouver Whitecaps and Nobby became his coach. Later he followed Giles to West Bromwich Albion to do a similar job at The Hawthorns, becoming a youth-team coach, a role he felt suited him best and gave him the most satisfaction.

Alex Ferguson heard about his good work at Albion and in 1989 after deciding that United's youth set-up needed overhauling, he invited Nobby to work with Brian Kidd and Archie Knox on youth development. He spent five years working at The Cliff but increasingly found he was becoming involved in administrative paperwork, which he didn't like.

By this time his colourful career and popularity had drawn him on to the after-dinner speaking circuit and he found it difficult to handle both demands. The result was that eventually he had to give up his United post to concentrate on the more lucrative speaking side of the game, and he certainly has plenty of tales to tell!

But there was still more drama to come in the life and times of Norbert Stiles when he suffered a heart attack in the summer of 2002. It was a major crisis in his life and perhaps a warning to slow down and take things a little easier. Or as Nobby puts it: "It was maybe a signal for the enjoyment of the rest of my days. A man couldn't have had a better wife or sons or friends, or memories of the one thing that had coloured all his days, the game of football, the great passion of the blood in my part of the town."

The little guy's nickname in his playing days among his team-mates was 'Happy', ironically enough for such a fierce fighter, and beyond all the controversial moments, that's how I will remember him as well.

The charismatic 'El Bandido' provided me with a great many stories, and can look back with pride on a colourful career, or as he puts it himself: "I thought of how I'd come to win a World Cup and a European Cup medal even though I was born a half-blind dwarf who was bombed by the Germans and run over by a trolley bus before I was one."

The powers-that-be left it a long time, but better late than never, and to be fair Nobby was late into the tackle on one or two occasions himself, but in her New Year's Honours list on the eve of the new century the Queen awarded him an MBE.

It was overdue and well deserved, and typically he accepted his honour with the words: "I'm absolutely delighted - and it's wonderful for my family."

NOBBY STILES - CAREER STATS

BORN:	Manchester
DATE OF BIRTH:	May 18 1942
JOINED UNITED:	September 1957
UNITED LEAGUE APPS:	311
GOALS:	17
INT. CAPS (England):	28
GOALS:	1

1961-1974

George
Best

If anyone ever doubted the charisma and magical mystique of George Best they only had to be around when he died aged only 59 on November 25, 2005. Although it had been 40 years since he had been lighting up the headlines with the tales of his achievements on the field and his romances off the field with the most beautiful girls in the country, the reaction was as if he had never been away.

Although we all knew George Best was living dangerously with a failing liver and transplant operation, it still came as a great shock to followers of football when we found that a guy who had lived so vividly in our minds for so long was no longer with us.

George had a star quality that made him as familiar to youngsters who never saw him actually play, as he was to all those mums and dads who had followed him in the sixties or who inevitably had read about him in the papers for one reason or another.

Clearly the memories had not faded as the news of his death broke. Admiration for the genius of George Best as a footballer came across in a flood of tributes. Two days after he died when United played at West Ham, the London crowd burst into spontaneous applause during the intended one-minute's silence.

The first game at Old Trafford came a few days later against

West Bromwich Albion in the Carling Cup and I was proud to be asked to present the on-field ceremony that preceded the match with the players of both teams lined up on the pitch with his family led by Dickie Best his father and Calum his son.

I think the club asked me because as the *Manchester Evening News* representative covering Manchester United for 37 years I had reported his debut, his triumphs and his tragedies right up until his departure from the game.

I explained that the club felt it was not an occasion for the applause that was becoming the way for admiring fans to express their appreciation, but that we would observe a silence because United fans had lost someone close and were still grieving. I said that the next home game three days later against Portsmouth would be the time to applaud and celebrate his brilliance.

Sir Alex Ferguson and visiting manager Bryan Robson laid wreaths beside a huge banner made by a group of fans reading 'George simply the Best', that was laid out in the centre circle.

I asked the crowd to hold aloft the posters they had been given bearing the face of George during the silence. Right around the ground the pictures looked across the pitch to make a sea of colour in a very emotional and moving tribute.

The pavement opposite the Old Trafford ground was turned into a shrine with a floral carpet over a hundred yards long and studded with scarves, shirts, photographs and memorabilia put there by fans representing not just United but many other clubs.

George had his well-documented troubles headlining his bizarre drinking and stormy personal life involving two marriages and countless relationships, but what came across for me in the days following his passing was a huge outpouring of love and affection to match the respect and admiration everyone felt for him as a footballer.

I am sure that people recognised that the person he hurt most by his behaviour was himself and so they forgave him. There are people who feel that he had a right to abuse his own liver, if that was his choice, though they weren't so sure he had been entitled to abuse someone else's following his life-saving transplant.

But he was the one who suffered in the end, dying at the age of 59 and as those horrific photographs of him lying on his deathbed as illness closed in showed only too vividly, it was hardly a peaceful passing.

Maybe football supporters felt he couldn't help himself and they understand that because we all have our failings. The one thing clear is that there was, and is, a great love for George Best as well as a fondness for his dazzling talents on the field of play.

Graham Williams, the Welsh international full-back who marked Best on his debut in 1963 against West Bromwich, was one of the guests at Old Trafford on the night we paid tribute to our fallen star, and he captured the essence of George when he said: "He would do his tricks and then he'd put his head down and his eyes would smile. Even if you won a tackle he would still smile."

As the wreath laid out on the turf that night spelt out, that was George being simply the Best, the man who despite the trials and tribulations put a smile on the face of football.

I sometimes wish I had had the nerve when I had the chance to have asked him if the real George Best would stand up, because he was a man of so many parts that I still have difficulty understanding what made him tick.

Obviously he was a footballer extraordinaire, certainly the most magical I have seen in my life as a football writer. We are all aware of the genius that has given us so many thrilling moments.

His tour de force against Benfica in Lisbon in 1966 when he destroyed the kings of Europe remains the highlight of my football reporting life.

His contribution to the victory that gave United the European

Cup two years later against Benfica at Wembley was similarly inspired.

The tales of his drinking, and the complications involved, have been just as colourfully reported and the dark side of his life adds to the mystery and puzzlement. I wonder also what exactly was his secret captivating so many gorgeous women throughout his life.

Then I think of the shy, insecure boy I met when he first came to Manchester. I remember his peculiar behaviour at times, such as walking out of a dinner party without saying a word to leave the rest of us wondering what had gone wrong. Clearly he was a complex man but one who inspired great love despite the flaws.

So my lasting memory of George is of the great outpouring of emotion at his passing. People paid him their respects for the magical moments he gave them on the pitch, but there was forgiveness too. They have been ready to love him in all his guises.

Sir Alex Ferguson spoke on the tribute day and told me: "It is ironic that West Bromwich Albion should be the first fixture at Old Trafford since George's passing after making his debut against them as a 17-year-old. He was a special player who always said he wanted to be remembered for his football, which is not difficult because he always gave such great joy to the game. He has left us with a million memories and in terms of football, all of them good. As well as his talent as a fantastic player, what remains in my mind is his courage. I can see him, even now, flying down the wing riding tackles and if he was brought down he simply got up again to start looking for the ball even more eagerly.

"George arrived on the scene at a liberated time with an explosion of music, *The Beatles*, stylish fashions and an altogether freer way of life. Some say he should have played longer for Manchester United but he played first-team football at Old Trafford for 10 years with a fine record of nearly 500 games and 200 goals, a phenomenal record considering he wasn't an out-and-out striker.

"Up until a few years ago I used to speak to him quite a lot. In those days he used to come to some of our games and I found him a really nice chap, a nice lad, unaffected by all his fame."

George certainly wouldn't have said boo to a goose when George Bishop, a lovely man and United's Belfast-based Northern Ireland scout, who had watched him play for Cregagh Boys Club, put him on the boat to Liverpool with another likely lad, Eric McMordie.

George hadn't made the Irish schoolboy team because he wasn't strong or big enough, and he didn't impress Mrs Mary Fullaway either when he was taken round to lodge at her council house home in Aycliffe Avenue, Chorlton-cum-Hardy.

"He looked more like a little jockey than a footballer. He was puny and petrified," declared his new landlady. He was homesick, too, and after a couple of days he and McMordie, without saying a word to anyone, caught the Ulster Prince night ferry back home to Belfast.

It wasn't long before Matt Busby and George's dad had agreed to persuade the boy to give it another try with Dickie Best insisting that United should find him a job in case football didn't work out.

So chief scout Joe Armstrong got him an office job with the Manchester Ship Canal Company because he was also a neat writer, working in the afternoons after training. That didn't last long, though, because George had started to enjoy the training and he was adjusting to his new footballing life.

Harry Gregg was one of the first to realise that there was a special talent among the juniors after volunteering to play with the kids one afternoon at The Cliff training ground. There came the moment when the boy he later described as "the skinny one" brought the ball up to him and scored by sending him diving the wrong way.

"A little later he wriggled clear again. I called his bluff because I had always prided myself on being able to make forwards do what I wanted in those circumstances but I got the same result, a humiliating dive with the ball at the other end of the goal.

"When George had the audacity to do it a third time I got up and joked: 'You do that again and I'll break your bloody neck, son.' I had a good laugh with George and the other lads, but when I left, the image of this pencil-thin lad with the breathtaking skills lingered on.

"Later that day I ran across Matt Busby at Old Trafford. We chatted briefly and as he turned to walk away. I asked him if he had seen the youngster, the little Belfast lad. He hadn't, and I suggested he take a look. A few days later we met again. 'I know the boy you mean. It's pity he's so small,' he said."

George's size was still being held against him and he was also painfully shy. In his early days he used to walk the long way round to the dressing rooms to avoid meeting people. He did his talking with the ball and he could make it sing beautifully.

But George stuck at it and worked his way through the A and B teams, making an occasional appearance with the reserves. He was a member of the team that won the FA Youth Cup in season 1963-64 and he was also given his League debut.

Aged 17 and four months he played against West Bromwich Albion at outside right facing the tough-tackling Graham Williams on September 14, 1963.

Best's debut wasn't a great performance but the Irishman made his mark and this was my verdict for the *Manchester Evening News*:

'There was also the prospect of young George Best to brighten up a dullish match. Despite the ordeal of a League debut after only three reserve matches, and a gruelling duel with full-back Graham Williams, and a painful ankle injury, he played pluckily and finished the game in style.

'None of the handicaps could disguise a natural talent. I know manager Matt Busby is looking forward to seeing this Belfast boy in a team with Law to help him. I agree – it is an exciting prospect that will brighten up the dullest of games.'

The next few years suggested I wasn't too far off the mark!

The game was won 1-0 with the scorer David Sadler, an England amateur at that time and of course George's house-mate with Mrs Fullaway in Chorlton. The team lined up:

Gregg, Dunne, Cantwell, Crerand, Foulkes, Setters, Best, Stiles, Sadler, Chisnall and Charlton.

Ian Moir won back the outside right position for the next game and George went back to the reserves. That Christmas, though, United suffered a humiliating 6-1 defeat against Burnley at Turf Moor and Busby promptly dropped the two wingers, Albert Quixall and Shay Brennan. At the same time a telegram was sent to Belfast recalling Best from his Christmas holiday at home.

Two days after the Boxing Day defeat at Turf Moor, with Best now on one wing and Willie Anderson taking over at outside left, United this time beat Burnley and by a big revenge score too, winning 5-1 with George among the scorers.

On the morning of the match I remember asking him if he was excited and the only reaction I got was a nonchalant shrug of the shoulders and a flat: "No." Even in those early days he was 'Mr Cool'. Right through his career he was always one of the last to get changed, often dashing into the dressing room after chatting to friends until half-an-hour before kick-off with the rest of the team already stripped and feeling the tension.

This time he stayed in the side until the end of the season and scored three goals in a total of 17 League appearances. He also shared in an FA Cup run that took them to the semi-finals, contributing a couple of goals and finally attracting the attention of the Northern Ireland selectors who had passed him over as a schoolboy.

It was as if they were trying to make up for lost time, giving him his first cap after just 21 first-team games, and playing on the right wing against Wales at Swansea in April 1964.

George went on to experience mixed fortunes on the international front because Northern Ireland weren't a particularly successful side in those days and he also missed a number of matches through injury. He missed out on playing in the finals of a major competition but nevertheless he did win 37 caps and score nine goals.

On the domestic front it was full steam ahead and after bringing in players like Noel Cantwell, Maurice Setters, John Connelly, Denis Law and Pat Crerand to augment the players beginning to roll off his own production line like George Best, Busby had a strong side again.

Best's first full season saw United win the Championship for the first time after Munich, George missing only one game and scoring 10 goals, not bad for the new boy! The Reds were firing on all cylinders with Denis Law at the peak of his powers, scoring 28 goals which along with 20 from David Herd, 15 by John Connelly and 10 from Bobby Charlton as well as 10 from Best, was fire-power second-to-none.

George Best represented the new look and appropriately enough had scored the opening goal in the 3-1 win against Arsenal that clinched the title on goal average from Leeds.

The 1964-65 championship side read:

Pat Dunne, Brennan, Tony Dunne, Crerand, Foulkes, Stiles, Connelly, Charlton, Herd, Law, Best.

The League success meant United were back in the European Cup for next season, and although they had played in the

European Cup Winners' Cup and the Fairs Cup, this the first time since the fateful trip to Belgrade seven years previously that they had appeared in the senior competition.

And what a momentous campaign it proved to be; they didn't even reach the final but it was the global launch pad for George Best. I can still see him now...slim, boyish, dark hair shining in the floodlights as he scythed through the Benfica defence leaving a trail of baffled Portuguese defenders in his wake. George was on his way to score one of the finest goals I have ever seen.

It was sheer poetry as he swept from the halfway line to weave his way past three white shirts before rounding goalkeeper Costa Pereira to clip the ball home for his second goal of the night and give United an aggregate lead in their European Cup quarter-final against the most powerful team in Europe.

I can remember leaping to my feet, so stunning was the fluid scoring movement and so remarkable the circumstances, as a 19-year-old stripling grabbed the football world by its ears with a tour de force that changed the perception of the game.

It was as audacious as it was unexpected. The Benfica players had been smiling when they had left the Old Trafford pitch after the first leg in Manchester, satisfied that United's one-goal lead from their 3-2 win was simply not good enough for the return leg in Lisbon's Estadio de Lus.

Bela Guttmann, the Benfica coach, looked confident too, as well he might. Benfica, twice European Cup winners who had won 18 and drawn one of their 19 European contests on their own ground, were successors to Real Madrid as kings of Europe.

It was a mighty record and as the Press boarded the charter plane in Manchester with Matt Busby and his players it was with some foreboding. The build-up to the game piled on the agony with the roads to the Stadium of Light so jammed that even the arrival of Italian referee Concetto Lo Bello was delayed.

Benfica added to the tension by presenting Eusébio with his Footballer of the Year trophy out on the pitch, a move that delayed the kick-off for 20 minutes with the United players left fretting in the tunnel.

Eventually they returned to their dressing room where, we learned later, Pat Crerand had shattered a huge mirror as he nervously kicked a ball about waiting for the action. His superstitious team-mates were not amused.

There was one, though, with ice in his veins. Nerves never troubled George Best and within six minutes of the start, unaffected by the rockets and shrieking 80,000 crowd, he leapt to head home Tony Dunne's free-kick and give his team an ideal start.

Then after another six minutes David Herd headed Harry Gregg's goal-kick down and into the path of Best, who streaked away on a solo run to score his remarkable goal and put United further ahead.

Then as if to show he was a team player as well as an individual artist he knocked on Denis Law's pass for John Connelly to make it three goals in an astounding opening quarter of an hour.

As Sir Matt said later: "George must have had cotton wool stuffed in his ears at the team talk because we were supposed to start cautiously."

The fact was the Eagles of Benfica had been plucked and though they pulled a goal back – and it was an own goal – United cruised to a 5-1 triumph with further goals from Pat Crerand and Bobby Charlton.

For all their domination in Europe, Benfica had been destroyed and you need look no further than the boy from Belfast for the inspiration and the delivery of a performance that created George Best the superstar and sent him on his way to become the game's first modern celebrity, pre-dating David Beckham by some 30 years.

George set the tone by buying a huge sombrero with a sixth sense telling him that it could be a useful prop looking for publicity to mark the opening of his boutique in Sale, a few miles from the ground, the following week.

It was an indication of much more to come as he stuck the hat on his head on arrival back at Manchester Airport to produce a picture that flew around the world.

The Press, already in love with the music of *The Beatles*, looked at his Ringo-style haircut and he arrived home christened forever as 'El Beatle.'

United were immediately installed as favourites to go all the way and win the European Cup, but they fell to Partizan Belgrade in the semi-finals and significantly Best played the first leg with a bad knee and then missed the return to undergo a cartilage operation. United without him were hardly in the hunt. When he went the magic went with him.

He was back the following season, though, to play through 1966-67 as an ever-present scoring 10 goals to help win the League again and put the Reds back into the European Cup. This time United made no mistake and went all the way, George enjoying his best-ever scoring year with 28 League goals from 41 appearances and proving an inspiration in Europe, especially in the testing semi-final against mighty Real Madrid.

Best scored at Old Trafford for a 1-0 win in the first leg and then set up the goal for a draw and aggregate winner in the second leg in Spain by scorching down the right wing to roll a pass into the path of Bill Foulkes, who for possibly the first time in his life had left his defensive duties at centre-half.

Foulkes was a stranger up front but he made no mistake for a goal which brought United their destiny in the 1968 final of the European Cup against Benfica at Wembley.

Normal time ended with the game level at 1-1 and it wasn't looking good for Busby's boys. Once again George Best produced the inspired moment. Just a minute into extra time he tore away to leave Cruz his marker trailing and then as Henrique came out he took the ball in a wide curve round the goalkeeper to clip it into an empty net.

Benfica were broken again and collapsed to lose 4-1 and give Matt Busby his dream just 10 years after the Munich air crash, a remarkable recovery.

The United manager knew just how much was due to George Best, and so did the football scribes. George was voted Player of the Year in Northern Ireland. The English writers gave him their award as well and six months later he was voted European Footballer of the Year, the youngest ever.

The following season saw George continue to deliver the goods with 19 goals from 41 appearances in the League as well as helping his club reach the semi-finals of the European Cup defending their title.

Cracks were appearing, though, and in the First Division they slipped to a finishing place of 11th. The club were heading for a period of change and troubled times for both Manchester United and George Best.

Sir Matt Busby, knighted by now and losing his mean streak – he was too kind-hearted to break up the team that had brought him his European triumph, retired. Wilf McGuinness was manager for 18 months, Frank O'Farrell was moved on after a similarly short stint in charge and the last thing George needed was this kind of inconsistent management. From being a hero he became a headache.

Season 1969-70 saw him twice sent off, the first time for kicking the ball out of referee Jack Taylor's hands, the second playing for his country when he was reported for throwing mud and spitting at referee Eric Jennings. He served a month's suspension for the first offence but amid much acrimony escaped punishment for the second with the support of the Irish FA, who wanted him available for the next international.

He still managed to score 15 goals to help United finish eighth, and indeed he scored 18 goals in each of his next two seasons, missing only four games. In those terms he was doing more than his fair share, but increasingly the player had the feeling that the club were going nowhere and that he was being asked to carry his fading team-mates on his shoulders.

Behind the scenes he was becoming increasingly difficult to manage. He failed to turn up for training on Christmas Day of 1970 and Wilf McGuinness found himself in a real dilemma when he caught George with a girl in his room a couple of hours before an FA Cup semi-final against Leeds. The situation called for disciplinary action but how can you drop your best player? Wilf played him but his behaviour was splitting the dressing room.

Frank O'Farrell once told me that he would never do any good at Old Trafford until the European stars had gone, that he needed time to develop his own team, which he wasn't given.

Tommy Docherty inherited the problem and persevered with patience, largely because once he had actually got George out on to the training pitch or in a game he was no problem. George still had his love for football; it was the bits in between that had become difficult.

The year 1972 was the beginning of the end when in January he walked out and missed a week's training. United ordered him to move back into digs with Mrs Fullaway instead of living on his own – except for girl friends – in the house he had had built in Cheshire's leafy Bramhall.

That didn't work and at the end of the season he skipped United's trip to Israel and turned up instead on the Costa del Sol, from where with the help of an avid media he held Press conferences claiming he was drinking a bottle of vodka a day.

"Mentally I am a bloody wreck, and I'm finished with football," he declared.

He changed his mind, came back and was given two weeks

suspension by his club who also told him to go and live with Pat Crerand and his family in an effort to get some order back into his life. That didn't last very long. "I think my kids drove him mad," says Pat.

Just before Christmas, 1972, United sacked O'Farrell and announced that Best was up for transfer and would not play for Manchester United again. The letter to him crossed with one from George announcing his retirement.

It was a sad end. He later played for Hibernian, Dunstable, Stockport County, Fulham and in America where he enjoyed a new lease of life in the slower-paced game played in the States.

The player bracketed his problems with the European Cup triumph and said: "It was as if everyone thought that winning the European Cup was the ultimate achievement. They were happy to relax and rest on their laurels. But to me, with a whole career ahead of me, it looked as if the future contained nothing but grafting about in the middle of the table, losing as many games as we won."

That's half the story but as we know more clearly now the demon drink was also taking its grip. His team-mates were divided in their views. One player who only caught the tail end of his career at Old Trafford said: "George thought he was the James Bond of soccer. He had everything he wanted and he pleased himself. He had money, girls and tremendous publicity. He lived from day-to-day and right to the end he got away with it when he missed training or ran away. So he didn't care. People made excuses for him. He didn't even have to bother to make them for himself. People talk about pressures and depressions. It was rubbish. He just didn't have any responsibilities, nothing to worry about at all. All kinds of people covered up for him, even the Press, and he was lucky to get away with it for so long."

A harsh judgement. Most of his peers were simply lost in admiration for his talent. Sir Bobby Charlton admired him, though he did get frustrated by him when they played together. He tells the story of how he used to wait for passes that never came and that George would use him as a dummy only to stay on a run with the ball. He did that in one match to leave Bobby starting to call him a greedy so-and-so only to find himself exploding: "What a great goal."

Denis Law says he loved playing with George and that without doubt he was the most gifted player he played with or against. "He had buckets of talent and - it may surprise some to hear this - he was also one of the best, most dedicated trainers I came across. Although he looked to be all skin and bone he was built like a whippet."

Alex Stepney believes it was his great fitness that enabled the player to carry on playing to such a high standard even after he had launched himself down the slippery slope of late nights and drinking too much.

As Nobby Stiles says in his book *After the Ball*: "George was a skinny kid when he arrived at Old Trafford and he never got to have much flesh on him. The strength sprang from deep inside him. He was a phenomenal trainer, and that was true whatever the situation. He could arrive unshaved and smelling of booze, but he was still brilliant when the work started. He was a lovely lad, too, there was no edge to him."

George was still only 27 when he walked away from his Manchester United career and opened a nightclub in Manchester that he called 'Slack Alice'.

As I wrote at the time: "Slack Alice had got her man early." It was a typical Besty gesture and a reflection of his life at the time which, as he would be the first to admit, was centred a great deal on birds and booze.

He was in the fast track all right with a stunning girlfriend Carolyn Moore, the reigning Miss Great Britain, on his arm, but the footballer who had become a household star reckoned that he couldn't go on in football any longer.

The rest of us found it hard to comprehend. Why should a young man who seemed to have everything want to throw it all away?

I had watched him blossom into a rare performer, who in my view still stands alone as the most gifted and exhilarating player I have ever seen, but once I had thought about it, I forgave him his early departure for a life with Slack Alice and her pals because when you analyse his career you realise George Best had more than paid his dues to the game.

He might have left it young, but he started young and played for 11 seasons in the First Division, packing more into his football career than the majority of professional players. If he had got into the first team at 21 and retired 11 years later at 32 nobody would have turned a hair. George just happened to live his career a little sooner than most!

So when people say that he threw away a great career they should remember that by the time he quit Old Trafford he had played 466 League, Cup and European games and scored 178 goals.

The other significant fact is that once he had established himself in the side he rarely missed a game. In fact in six of his seasons when he was in full flow he made either 40, 41 or an ever-present 42 league appearances each year.

That's hardly the career of a fly-by-night and when you consider the knocks he took and the magic he so often created I believe he was entitled to call it a day when he felt he had had enough.

Even when he went to America he continued to play more football than is popularly supposed. He played on for five more years with Los Angeles Aztecs, Fort Lauderdale Strikers and San Jose Earthquakes to make 139 appearances and score 54 goals. Not exactly a lightweight in the States either!

In terms of providing entertainment he definitely packed in more than most. He transported so many of us to the heights of delight...and I'm not referring to the girls, including a Miss World as well as a Miss Great Britain, who had flocked to swoon at the feet of a cult figure leading soccer into the Swinging Sixties.

Those final photographs of him portrayed a sad image as he lay in bed over the last few days ravaged by illness, gaunt and clearly at death's door but I prefer to remember him as the good-looking, fresh-faced boyo who took our game by storm one frenzied night in Lisbon.

GEORGE BEST - CAREER STATS

BORN:	Belfast
DATE OF BIRTH:	May 22 1946
JOINED UNITED:	August 1961
UNITED LEAGUE APPS:	361
GOALS:	137
INT. CAPS (N. Ireland):	37
GOALS:	9

1962-1973

Denis Law

Denis Law has long reigned as The King following his brave exploits for Manchester United in the Sixties, but now he has been crowned monarch of the glens as well.

A *Daily Record* newspaper poll a year or two ago voted him the greatest Scottish player of all time, coming out on top ahead of formidable rivals for the honour like Kenny Dalglish and the popular Jim Baxter.

Naturally the 'Lawman' was also voted into Scotland's all-time greatest team and he was presented with his award by former team-mate Sir Bobby Charlton at a Hampden Park ceremony attended by Chancellor Gordon Brown.

Sir Alex Ferguson, who was voted the leading Scottish manager, delighted the tartan army when he claimed that the greatest-ever Scotland team would always beat an all-time England side. Referring to Law and Dalglish as a strike partnership 'made in heaven,' he said: "Dalglish or Law would score in the first minute, then they would give the ball to Jimmy "Jinky" Johnstone and the other lot wouldn't get it back off him until the final whistle."

The 60-year-old Law replied: "At this stage of my life it's fantastic to receive such an honour. When I think of the great players who have graced the Scottish jersey, and I have played with many of them like Jim Baxter and Kenny Dalglish, then I am thrilled that the *Record* readers have chosen me."

Even in his early days with Huddersfield there was an arrogance about Law's football that suggested he could perform on a bigger stage, and not long after his attempt to buy him as a youth player, Matt Busby, enjoying a brief spell as manager of Scotland, capped him against Wales at Ninian Park, Cardiff, on October 18th, 1958. He marked the occasion by scoring in a 3-0 win. Still only 18 he was the youngest to play for the full Scotland team after Bob McColl in 1899.

In all he played 55 times for Scotland for a tally of 30 goals, an impressive international career but one that Denis looks back on with some regret.

"Injuries didn't help me very much in my international career. I played a few times when I wasn't fully fit. You can get away with it at club level but not in internationals. I'm very proud to have played for Scotland. There is nothing quite like pulling on a Scottish jersey, but I would have liked to have done more."

His international career spanned all his clubs with even a call-up when he was back at Manchester City for a second and final stint. A tally of nine goals in 24 appearances for City earned him a place at the end of the season in the Scotland squad for the World Cup in West Germany in 1974.

Denis played in the opening group game against Zaire. Scotland won 2-0 but he was dropped in favour of Willie Morgan and it was his last international appearance. His retirement from football came not long after.

The fact that Scottish fans have looked back nearly 40 years to find their favourite Hampden Hero speaks volumes for the enduring memory of a fearless forward who has also remained close to the hearts of Manchester United followers.

Manchester remained his home and he is as popular as ever. The last few years has seen two books published recording his life and times.

The first was his autobiography written with Bob Harris, and the other was by Brian Hughes, author, a boxing coach and ardent United fan who gives us a supporter's perspective. Naturally both books are called *The King*. What else?

In the pantheon of United greats of that era, Bobby Charlton was admired, George Best was feted, but the Lawman was the people's champion because he brought together flair and fire.

The Stretford-Enders found it easy to identify with a player whose determination was so obvious. He was slightly built, but there was an aggression in his play that made him a hero and which at times could bring him into confrontation with opponents as well as referees.

It all added to his status, though, and his followers certainly liked the streak of villainy which ran through his football and which saw him serve two lengthy six-week suspensions in the course of his career.

His tendency to get into trouble with referees undoubtedly prevented the sensitive souls of the English football writers from ever making him their Footballer of the Year, but the more worldly European reporters took a broader view and voted him the European Player of the Year in 1964, and deservedly so.

The United fans certainly loved his willingness to fly into the thick of the action. He was daring, cocky, impudent and abrasive, which together with his lightning-quick football, his perception for being in the right place at the right time, and his prolific goalscoring, was an explosive mix.

He flourished in front of goal, where his scoring rate made him the most deadly marksman of all the famous players to perform on the Old Trafford stage.

Few from that time will forget the Law trademark as he signalled his goals to the crowd, punching the air and wheeling away with arm raised, his hand clutching his sleeve, save for the one finger pointing to the sky to acknowledge the strike. The terrace fans would rise to his salute as to a gladiator of old.

His strike rate was phenomenal in League, FA Cup and Europe. He scored 171 goals from 305 League games (plus 4 sub appearances), 34 FA Cup goals in 44 appearances and 28 goals in 33 European games. When Wembley beckoned he was particularly lethal. He once scored six for Manchester City in an FA Cup tie against Luton, only to see them chalked off the record when the game was abandoned because of a waterlogged pitch.

Sir Bobby Charlton scored a record 199 times but it took him 604 games to do it, while for all his magic, George Best had a ratio of 137 goals from 361 appearances. David Herd hit 144 goals in 263 appearances, impressive but nobody could quite touch the Lawman.

In more recent times, Ruud van Nistelrooy was clearly well on his way towards challenging Law's return, but failed to last the Old Trafford course and he was transferred to Real Madrid. The Dutchman had already matched Law's European total by scoring 28 goals and, significantly, had done it in four fewer games. Nistelrooy's top-flight strike rate was also impressive with 81 appearances yielding a superb 62 goals, but he still had some way to go to match Law's career tally.

But of course statistics only tell half the story, and don't totally explain why he was so lionised by the crowd. What the fans loved so much was the way he scored so many of his goals with spectacular overhead and scissors kicks along with whiplash headers so powerful that these days he is now paying the price with problems to his neck.

He jumped so high at times and hung there so long that it looked as if he had a skyhook. He was lean and hungry with his courage never in question. Speedy over two or three yards, his reflexes were razor sharp. Yet few would have predicted a glittering career looking at Denis Law as a youngster.

Born in Aberdeen the youngest of seven children, life was fairly hard. His father worked on the fishing trawlers and there were few luxuries. A pal gave him his first pair of football boots so that he could play for the school U11 team. He remembers his first new pair bought by his mum when he was 13.

"I caught the tram and went down to the city on a cloud. I bought myself a pair of Hotspur boots. They had big ankle protectors and were as hard as a brick. I can remember sitting on the sink with my feet in a basin of water to soften the leather," he explains.

Denis graduated to play for the Aberdeen schoolboys and was picked on one occasion as a reserve for the Scottish Schools team, but he was competing against bigger boys at a stage of development when size matters, and he was a titch!

Nevertheless he came to the attention of Archie Beattie who sent him down from Aberdeen for a trial with his brother Andy, the manager of Huddersfield.

Bill Shankly, who was then in charge of Huddersfield's reserves before becoming manager, said later: "He looked like a skinned rabbit. My first reaction was to say get him on the next train home."

But Huddersfield still saw enough to take him on to their ground staff as an apprentice in April 1955, and he was soon in Huddersfield's youth team where he caught the eye of Matt Busby in an FA Youth Cup tie against Manchester United. Huddersfield lost, but Busby after the game offered Andy Beattie £10,000 for his 16-year-old forward, a remarkably big offer for such a young player.

The bid was turned down because Huddersfield had other plans and on Christmas Eve, 1956, their promising apprentice was given his League debut at inside right against Notts County aged 16 years and 10 months, the youngest player Huddersfield have ever fielded.

A life in professional football had not been easy for the young Law. Apart from the lack of physique, he had also been forced to play with one eye closed because it was 'lazy' and meant he had a squint.

An operation put that right and as he explained in his book: "I cannot emphasise enough what an incredible moment in my life that was. It completely changed things for me. Suddenly I had the wherewithal to look people, literally, straight in the eye, something I had never been able to do with any confidence before.

"I returned to Huddersfield after a couple of weeks convalescence, and it was a great feeling just to go into the ground with the rest of the lads and be normal. Wow! And I could now play football with both eyes open."

In December 1959, Bill Shankly left to become manager of Liverpool, and speculation mounted that the up-and-coming Law would also be leaving, with Everton, Arsenal, Chelsea and Glasgow Rangers all reported as interested. It was in fact Manchester City who landed him, paying £55,000 on March 15th, 1960, a British record transfer fee.

He had only made 81 League appearances for Huddersfield who were a Second Division club of course, but his potential, even at that stage, was enormous.

Denis had only been at Maine Road for two seasons before the chance of a big profit proved too tempting for City, who would have found it extremely difficult anyway to have stood in his way when Italy came calling. He had scored 21 goals in 44 League appearances, despite not playing in a very good side. City had Bert Trautmann in goal but Denis only rated Ken Barnes and George Hannah as top players and it was clear that the threat of relegation was never far away. Denis made a friend for life in Ken Barnes but Italian football at that time was a huge attraction for any ambitious player good enough to feel he could make it, and the young Law never lacked confidence.

John Charles had led the way and the Italians had a very personable scout called Gigi Peronace whose job was to seek out the best English football had to offer. Not that Denis needed much persuasion after being contacted by the fast-talking Gigi.

"I knew that if I stayed at City I faced the prospect of a continued fight against relegation. I wanted to go to Italy. There was just this feeling that it was the place to be," explained Denis.

The financial attraction was considerable when Torino sent Peronace to offer him a £5,000 signing-on fee plus bonuses such as £200 for a win, a lira lure that compared well with the maximum wage of £20 a week. City collected a record £110,000 fee for his transfer on June 9, 1961, but the Italian move proved a disaster.

The dream became a nightmare. The Italians talked big money but promises didn't always materialise. Football over there was alien, too. Although Torino also signed Joe Baker from Hibs so that they had each other for English company, they were bored and lonely. They found the Press and the fans intrusive and it seemed they were always in trouble and being fined by the club for minor misdemeanours.

Joe Baker so disliked being taken away to training camps in the mountains above Turin in preparation for matches that he went on a hunger strike until, much to the delight of the other players, the practice was abandoned. Their most horrendous experience was when Joe turned his new car over going the wrong way round a roundabout and suffered head injuries, with Denis fortunate to avoid being crushed.

The final experience that tipped Denis over the edge came when he was pulled off the pitch in a Cup tie and accused of not trying because, they said, he was saving himself for a Scotland international that was coming up. Torino refused to release him and Denis decided he needed to get back home.

"I realised I had made a ghastly mistake. I'm not one for the high life but it was like a prison," he says. Denis simply ignored Torino's refusal to let him play in the Scotland match and stormed out, even leaving all his clothes behind.

Back in Scotland for the game Denis contacted Busby and

was delighted when the United manager intimated that if he became available he would be bidding. Gigi was now summoned to work a Law transfer the other way. After a typical Italian complication with Torino attempting to sell him to Juventus for £160,000, Gigi finally smoothed the way for him to join Manchester United for a record £115,000 with Denis a sadder but wiser - and probably better - footballer.

Despite his problems in Turin he had still done his stuff out on the field by scoring 10 goals in 27 League matches, a more than useful contribution in Italian football and especially when you consider that just four more goals would have made him the Italian League's top scorer.

On July 12th, 1962, after a lengthy chase by Matt Busby, he arrived at Manchester United for an eventful first season in 1962-63 that saw United flirt with relegation. It was only five years after the Munich air crash with Busby still trying to rebuild the team. Denis naturally played up front alongside David Herd and though they finished a lowly 19th there was nothing wrong with the strike force. Denis immediately contributed 23 League goals from 38 appearances, a goodly return playing in a new team, while Herd weighed in with his customary 19 goals.

Denis was on song in the FA Cup, too, scoring a hat-trick against his first English club, Huddersfield, in the third round and also scoring against Chelsea and Southampton in the semi-final to reach Wembley and meet Leicester City in the final.

By this time Busby had bought Pat Crerand from Glasgow Celtic to improve the service to the front men and the revamped side came into its own in the final. Leicester, going well in the League, were clear favourites against a side that the Division One table told you was struggling.

Against all the odds, and with a show of things to come, United sparkled that day at Wembley and ran Leicester ragged on their way to a handsome 3-1 win. Denis rates it as one of the

greatest games he played for United and says: "I can see Paddy Crerand hitting me with a perfect ball from the left wing. I turned quickly and shot past Gordon Banks' right hand. It was, the first goal, and one I had always dreamed of scoring at Wembley. David Herd scored the other two goals in a match that proved to be a turning point along the road to recovery after Munich.

The following season saw everything click together with more consistency for United to finish runners-up in the League, reach the final of the FA Cup again and score a lot of goals in the European Cup Winners' Cup before a shock defeat against Sporting Lisbon. They now had a defence to match their fearsome firepower, which saw Law hit a fabulous goal-a-game rate of 30 in 30 appearances.

This was the new United who did even better the following season, winning the 1964-65 Championship on the back of 28 goals from Law, 20 again from Herd, 15 by John Connelly, 10 from Bobby Charlton and with another 10 by the fast emerging George Best.

They again reached the FA Cup semi-finals and enjoyed a good run in the Inter-Cities Fairs Cup. Manchester United were certainly swinging as they moved through the Sixties and qualified as champions to play in the European Cup in season 1965-66.

They gave a good account of themselves until they lost to Partizan Belgrade in the semi-finals. They finished fourth in the League, which meant they could concentrate on the Championship the following season without any European involvement. Early exits from the two domestic cup competitions also helped by leaving them completely free of distractions and they made no mistake. They were champions again with the chance to make amends for the unexpected semi-final flop against Partizan. Denis Law had once more led the way as top scorer with a tally of 23 goals backed up by Herd,

Charlton and Best in their all-star attack.

So to season 1967-68 and this time they swept through Hibernians (Malta), Sarajevo and Gornik Zabrze before pulling out all the stops to beat Real Madrid in a thrilling semi-final.

Denis Law had struggled with a knee injury for most of the European campaign and was in hospital for a knee operation when his team-mates beat Benfica 4-1 in extra time at Wembley for United to become the first English club to win the European Cup.

Although he was naturally disappointed to miss out on such an important occasion, at least he had finally got his knee sorted out. The problem had been the bane of his life and he had deeply resented implications that the injury was more in his mind than his knee! As he describes it in his book: "In England, racehorses received better treatment than we did.

"Football's idea of curing an injury was to use cortisone injections. When injected into your body it disguised pain for three or four hours, converted into cortisol and influenced the nutrition and growth of connective tissues.

"The advice now is not to have more than one a month, with a maximum of three or four during the course of a year, and to avoid excessive movement or stress on the joint for about a week, but we were injected and told to go straight out and play.

"During those years of my knee injury I seemed to have one every week. I used to come into the dressing room at half-time with my knee aching and throbbing and I would sit in the big bath with a hosepipe spraying cold water on it in an effort to deaden the pain. That was the extent of my treatment. Then I would get out of the bath and go out and play.

"The most expensive player on United's books, and that was how I was treated. And not just me, I hasten to add, everybody was treated the same. Do that for a season or two seasons, just to deaden the pain, with regular cortisone injections, and it will begin to take its toll. It was and should have been unacceptable, but we put up with it without demur.

"I just didn't think long-term when it came to my career. The culture at that time was to be ready for the next match whatever the problem, but because of the severity of my knee injury, this was not lengthening my career, it was shortening it. By deliberately deadening the pain month after month, I was doing long-term damage.

"Everyone would be delighted because I had got through another game, and then it was back on the treadmill, not training but having treatment for another week, and then back on to the pitch for the next match - and this was the pattern for over two years. George Best was into all that as well for a long time with his bad knee: injections, hot and cold water, and aspirins. Looking back on it now, it's hard to believe. Nowadays clubs have realised how valuable their playing assets are; the training ground at Manchester United is just phenomenal, with physios, doctors, medical equipment, ultrasound - everything a finely-tuned athlete needs.

"My knee problem got much worse in 1967. At the time I was having trouble with both the club doctor and the team physio because I was seeing my own osteopath, Mr Millwood, to whom I had been recommended by a friend of mine. I'd gone private several months earlier because nothing seemed to be easing my pain, but in those days an osteopath was not deemed to be a legitimate man; in fact, he was considered to be something of a witch doctor.

"They were so wrong. Mr Millwood looked after me brilliantly and gave me what the others couldn't. He was so helpful I used him for several years, paying for it myself. When the club found out what I was doing and expressed their anger, my attitude was: 'It's my knee, it's my life, it's my career, it's my livelihood, and if you are not going to do anything about it then I've no choice but to go and get someone else to look after me.'"

United even insisted that Law went on a close-season tour to

Australia which he believes was the reason that in season 1967-68 he played only 23 League games, many of them when he wasn't fully fit. He reckons he had more treatment in that one season than a player should have in a career, and that the club insisted they couldn't find anything wrong and that it was all in his mind.

"It's amazing that we weren't looked after better. It often felt like that Jane Fonda film, *They Shoot Horses, Don't They?* about dancers who danced in competitions until they dropped. The same could have applied to footballers," he says.

A visit to a Harley Street specialist finally came up with the possibility that the surgeon who had supposedly taken out his cartilage when he was playing for Huddersfield had failed to extract the entire piece of gristle and that this had been knocked loose and was the source of the aggravation. Denis had played just three games in the European Cup that season and was finally in hospital for a much-needed knee operation when his team-mates ran out against Benfica at Wembley.

It was only supposed to be an exploratory operation, but they pulled out a piece of floating cartilage, put it in a jar and gave it to him. It was an inch-and-a-half long.

And they said it had all been in his mind!

As for the final, the nurses at St Joseph's were United supporters and a few of his pals came in too, and along with the nurses they watched the match in his room and on a very emotional night they ended up worse for wear.

Said Denis: "I took the congratulations from my friends, the nursing staff and other patients, but it wasn't about me; it was about Sir Matt, a decade after he had lain on what he must have thought was his deathbed. The cheers were soon mixed with tears as Matt Busby finally held aloft the European Cup."

After recovering from his knee operation he returned to action to make 30 League appearances in season 1968-69 and score 14 goals, but really his best days were behind him and George

Best had taken over as the major scoring threat. The team were heading for traumatic times, too, with Sir Matt Busby looking to step down from front-line management.

Wilf McGuinness took over as manager for 18 months, Busby returned for a spell and then Frank O'Farrell became manager for a year-and-a-half. It was a difficult time for the new coaches as an ageing team started to unravel, and not easy for players who had known better days of course.

Then Tommy Docherty breezed in and despite a promise to his fellow Scot that there would be a place for him on the coaching staff at the end of his playing career, gave him a free transfer at the end of season 1972-73.

Even the manner of being told he was no longer wanted wasn't done in a very nice way, and I unwittingly played a part in the upset. Denis was in Aberdeen visiting family when the Doc gave me the list of retained players with the names of those he had decided to release and naturally I splashed the news of Denis Law's pending departure in that Saturday night's 'Football Pink'.

Television picked up the story and the first Denis knew of it was that evening when it came up on his television screen. Not a very sensitive end to such a distinguished career, but then it couldn't have been very dignified for David Sadler at the start of his career when he was Denis' understudy either.

"After my initial breakthrough, for several years I would come in and play when the likes of Denis or David Herd were not available," explains David. " The Lawman spent a lot of the time in the treatment room but, before a match, Matt Busby would never state that Denis wasn't going to be fit. If there was a doubt it was always left until as late as possible before making a decision.

"After all if you said at the start of the week that Law was out then you could take some off the crowd. Matt wouldn't miss a trick. So quite often I wouldn't know until a couple of hours before a game that Denis had failed a fitness test. So as we walked out on to the pitch they would announce that Sadler was replacing Law, and believe me, it was a great welcome to walk out to some 60,000 people booing because I had replaced their hero. Not that I could blame them - I would have booed, too!"

Football can be a harsh and cruel business sometimes.

As a free agent Denis crossed Manchester to play one final season for City. He made 24 League appearances and scored nine goals, with his last one never to be forgotten because at the time it looked as if it could send Manchester United down into the Second Division. In the last-but-one game of season 1973-74 United met City at Old Trafford and there was no score when a cross came into the United goalmouth. Denis standing with his back to goal casually back-heeled the ball which went past Alex Stepney to give his old club a 1-0 defeat. It was a goal later described by Denis as a fluke. Certainly there was no rushing over to kiss the club badge in front of your supporters for this one. Denis walked back to the centre circle looking as if he had accidentally stabbed his best friend in the back!

Actually he needn't have worried, because both United's rivals in distress won, which meant the Reds were going down to the Second Division anyway. Nevertheless it was hardly a career final goal to commemorate!

So that was it apart from the short-lived World Cup campaign in West Germany and when Denis learned from Tony Book, the City manager, that he didn't figure in his first-team plans for the following season the Lawman decided to retire, though he does now regret that he didn't play on for longer, perhaps in America.

"If I have a lasting regret, it's that I quit football a year or so too early - you are a long time retired - and that afterwards I didn't take that coaching course which would have kept me in the football world. I confess that I do look back and feel a little unfulfilled, but I'm afraid it's too late now."

Not that Denis is anything but cheerful when you bump into

him around Old Trafford or at the social functions of the Association of Former Manchester United Players. He's a keen supporter of the Association and has retained his links with the club he served so well, particularly with his daughter Di, now the popular media officer at Old Trafford.

Retirement from football saw him stay on in Manchester, settled with Diana his wife and five children. He became a familiar voice on radio and television as well as joining Francis Lee's paper manufacturing business for a while and involvement with several other business ventures.

He still makes celebrity appearances and occasionally joins the speaking circuit to talk about his career at sportsman's functions. He still lives in Bowdon and plays golf at Northenden.

Not so long ago he had to battle with prostate cancer but with typical courage he tackled it head-on and even went public, which is not generally something he enjoys. He agreed to an interview in the local paper in order to spread the word that it is a problem that can be beaten. He won though like the king he is, and looks back fondly on his 11 years with Manchester United.

He sums up: "It was the swinging Sixties in soccer as well as in the entertainment world with *The Beatles* and I think we saw football at its best. I was privileged to play in a great side. It was a beautiful team to play in with players like Paddy Crerand, Bobby Charlton, Nobby Stiles and George Best. For five years it was a joy for the entertainment and goals. We always felt that if the opposition scored one, we could score two, and if they got two we could score three. It didn't always work out that way, but that was the feeling, and it was all very special for me."

He was special to Manchester United fans, too, not least to Sir Matt Busby who told me some years ago: "Denis Law was the most expensive signing I ever made, but on achievement he turned out to be the cheapest. The Italians dragged me and my chairman all over Europe before we were able to complete the signing, and at one time I was so angry at the way we were being treated that I almost pulled out of the deal.

"I'm extremely glad that I didn't. Once we had got Denis to Old Trafford I knew that we had the most exciting player in the game. He was the quickest-thinking player I ever saw, seconds quicker than anyone else. He had the most tremendous acceleration, and could leap to enormous heights to head the ball with almost unbelievable accuracy, and often with the power of a shot.

"He had the courage to take on the biggest and most ferocious opponents, and his passing was impeccable. He was one of the most unselfish players I have ever seen. If he was not in the best position to score he would give the ball to someone who was.

"When a chance was on for him, even only a half-chance, or in some cases no chance at all for anyone but him, whether he had his back to goal, was sideways on, or the ball was on the deck or up at shoulder height, he would have it in the net with such power and acrobatic ability that colleagues and opponents alike could only stand and gasp.

"No other player scored as many 'miracle' goals as Denis Law."

DENIS LAW - CAREER STATS	
BORN:	Aberdeen
DATE OF BIRTH:	February 24 1940
JOINED UNITED:	August 1962
UNITED LEAGUE APPS:	309
GOALS:	171
INT. CAPS (Scotland):	55
GOALS:	30

Duncan Edwards (right) celebrates victory at Bournemouth in the FA Cup quarter-final, March 1957 with John Berry (left) and manager Matt Busby

Bobby Charlton (right) fires towards the Everton goal at Old Trafford

Bobby Charlton shows his 'balancing ball' prowess for the cameras

Above: Bobby Charlton leads Manchester United out, followed by George Best, while (below) Nobby Stiles makes his point after a team-mate has been scythed down

Nobby Stiles makes his entrance in the famous red shirt

George slides in against Liverpool at Anfield, with
goalkeeper Tommy Lawrence standing in his way

An Everton defender is warned after George Best has been stopped in his tracks

Above: It's the Leeds United 3 against George Best, and (below) collecting his 1968 European Footballer Of The Year award at Old Trafford

Above: George Best looks on as Denis Law fires a shot in pre-match, while (below) Denis prepares a shot of a different kind at a pre-season photocall

Denis Law lifts the League Championship trophy, with Bobby Charlton (left), George Best (second right) and Bill Foulkes (right) watching on

Above and opposite: Some of the silverware lifted during Bryan Robson's United career - the FA Cup, in 1985 (opposite) and the 1991 European Cup Winners' Cup

Bryan Robson leads United out for the final time, and (below) the players salute an Old Trafford legend as he bids farewell to the club

Eric Cantona is mobbed by fans as the long-awaited title celebrations begin, May 1993

A young autograph hunter in Hungary tries his luck with Eric, September 1993

Eric lifts the Premier League trophy in 1994

Eric Cantona in relaxed mood before the awards ceremony in which he
was to collect the 1996 Football Writers' Player Of The Year trophy

Skipper Eric Cantona leads United out ahead of the 1996
FA Charity Shield date with Newcastle at Wembley

David Beckham opens the scoring in the 4-1 victory over Charlton at
Old Trafford in May 2003 that clinched the Premier League crown

Above: David Beckham fires a free-kick towards goal while (below) he
challenges Ryan Giggs for England, against Wales in September 2005

Above: Ryan Giggs and Gary Neville lift the 2006-07 Premier League crown, and (below) star man Cristiano Ronaldo in action during the campaign

Sir Alex Ferguson shows his disgust after a late challenge on Ronaldo
in the FA Cup semi-final victory over Watford, April 2007

1981-1994

Bryan Robson

It was Sir Bobby Robson who dubbed him 'Captain Marvel', and with good cause, because Bryan Robson at the peak of his career was the England manager's best player by a mile. Indeed there was a tendency to regard England as a one-man team, and certainly when he wasn't playing there was a big hole in the team.

I well remember the England Press conferences at the 1988 European Championships in Germany when the fitness or otherwise of the skipper was the first item that came up for discussion. It was a disastrous campaign for our national side and but for Bryan's efforts they may well have completely fallen apart. The manager was pilloried as a 'plonker' and the tabloid papers were screaming for him to go, but nobody pointed a finger at the captain because everyone recognised that he was the one big redeeming feature. He was certainly England's best player and one of the few to come home with his reputation still intact.

Carrying a team was nothing new to Bryan Robson. The 1980s were not Manchester United's best years, certainly not in Championship terms where the League and European competition were dominated by Liverpool. United made their mark in the FA Cup, but I shudder to think how the Reds would have fared had it not been for the way they were shored up by the indefatigable driving power of their captain.

I remember from my days covering United for the *Manchester Evening News* that around that time Dr. Ray Kirby sent me a statistical analysis of how the team had performed with Robson playing compared with their record without him. Dr. Kirby told me: "United have won 0.45 points a game more with Bryan Robson in the team, which is equivalent of 20 points a season. They simply score more goals and concede fewer with Robson in the side."

No match sums up for me the total commitment of Bryan Robson than the night they played Barcelona at Old Trafford in the quarter-finals of the 1984 European Cup Winners' Cup. The captain felt he had let the team down in the first leg in Spain when he had missed chances and the side had come home with a 2-0 defeat. Nothing had gone right for the Reds. Graeme Hogg had desperately tried to clear after 35 minutes but only succeeded in slicing the ball into his own net. It looked as if United would keep the defeat down to just Hogg's error but in the dying seconds Rojo fired a fierce shot to make it 2-0.

Robson played the after-match Press conference like a true captain, immediately accepting responsibility for the defeat by pointing to the scoring chances he had missed. He insisted that Hogg should not be made the scapegoat because, he argued, the real culprit was himself as a senior player and the opportunities he had spurned. He promised that he, personally, would make amends in the return match at Old Trafford. Even so, not many United fans gave their side much of a chance against a very good Barcelona side that at that time included the great Diego Maradona. But Bryan Robson was as good as his word and set about the second leg as if he was on a personal crusade, which as far as he was concerned he was!

United won a corner through the persistence of Arnold Muhren after 22 minutes. Ray Wilkins dipped his corner-kick to the near post where Norman Whiteside outjumped the Spanish defence to head the ball across the goalmouth. In came the unstoppable Robson, stooping to head home and pull an early goal back. The crowd took off and Barcelona grew a little anxious. Alonso turned the ball back to his goalkeeper, Urruti, but was weak with his kick. Whiteside, Wilkins and Remi Moses roared forward to create panic in the Spanish defence. Once again it was Robson to the fore, pouncing on the loose ball to force it home and level the tie on aggregate. Just two minutes later, Frank Stapleton grabbed the winner with a rocket of a shot and United had won 3-2 to go through to their first European semi-final for 15 years.

Bryan Robson had been the man inspired he promised and at the end of the game supporters broke on to the pitch to hoist the skipper on to their shoulders and drape a Union Jack flag round his shoulders to create an iconic picture I and many more will never forget. It was a performance that prompted the old master, Sir Matt Busby to say: "The memories came flooding back", and I'm sure one of them must have been from his early days in the European Cup when United came back from another Spanish trip on the back of a 5-3 defeat in Bilbao only to win the return leg 3-0 at Maine Road. It was a comparable revival and I'm not surprised that Robson has since looked back and declared that beating Barcelona in 1984 had to be one of the greatest moments of his career.

He recalls: "I have never heard noise from the crowd like it. It seemed to get louder as the game went on and it made us feel that there was no way we could let anyone down. Sometimes during a game there will be quiet moments, but not that night. I am sure the passion behind the noise had an effect on the Spanish.

"Barcelona may have been used to playing in front of bigger crowds – their own stadium held far more than Old Trafford – but they had never heard anything like the roar which greeted them that night. Because of this we sensed from the start that we were in with a chance and we were right.

"Although we were 2-0 down and Barcelona had world stars like Maradona and Berndt Schuster in their side, we knew they were not invincible. What we needed was an early goal, and once we got that, the advantage began to swing our way.

"I thought Barcelona had been a bit lucky in the first leg. They took the lead through an own goal that left young Graeme Hogg devastated, and the rest of us felt the same way when they scored their second right at the death. Apart from that we held our own in the Nou Camp, and I was the one with a guilt complex for throwing away two glorious scoring opportunities. I said afterwards that I owed the lads something after those missed chances and was delighted I was able to play my part at Old Trafford.

"I was not alone. Everybody did their bit. From the fans who shouted until they were hoarse to the lads who ran themselves into the ground. Gary Bailey pulled off important saves, Arnie Muhren and Ray Wilkins controlled midfield, and Remi Moses kept such a close watch on Maradona I'm sure they had to stop him from boarding the plane back to Spain when the game was over!

"I have many fond memories of my time at Old Trafford, and Barcelona figures in them more than once, but the magical night when we did what they all thought impossible will stay with me forever. If you were one of those who shouted us to victory that night, thanks for the memory."

The ability of Bryan Robson to put mind over matter was always a constant thread running through his playing career; indeed it was sheer willpower that enabled him to push himself through the pain barrier of his many injuries to reach the high levels that made him such a forceful character for both club and country.

The remarkable thing is that though Captain Marvel delivered daring deeds on the football field, he wasn't blessed with the physique of Superman. Indeed, the physiotherapist who tended his injuries for most of the player's time at Old Trafford reckons a more accurate name for Bryan Robson would be 'Captain Miracle'.

"Throughout his career the demands he put on his body outweighed its capability. He busted a gut all the time and even in training at the end of his playing career he wanted to lead the pack and very often did," says Jim McGregor, United's physio under first Ron Atkinson and then Sir Alex Ferguson until going into private practice in St. John Street, Manchester.

"Bryan is mentally the strongest player I have ever seen, quite unbelievable. His injuries are well documented but I could fill half a book with the ones he has covered up because eventually he became sensitive about being hurt once again. Very often he's played when he shouldn't have done out of pride and perhaps stubbornness.

"The man really had no right to play for as long as he did at the top level until he was 37 because basically he just hadn't got the physique to have lasted so long. The reason he did last and became such a great player was because he drove himself beyond normal limits.

"He played such a tough, hard game not because he had a tough, hard body but because he put mind over physical hurt. Tests when he was playing amazingly showed Bryan Robson just didn't have real muscle power. He was the same weight and height as Paul Ince and Roy Keane, but he didn't have their muscle strength and tone.

"Bryan's strength came from within. He was still playing at the age of 37 because he was one of the few players who could run 40 miles when there were only 30 miles left in the tank. He had such a burning desire. He never gave up. If it had been down to physical make-up he would have retired two or three years before he did. It was sheer will-power that saw him through towards the end. People talked about him driving the team, and he did, but he drove himself hardest of all.

"You expect a midfield player to get more injuries than players in other positions. The position is more susceptible because midfielders are hit from the front, back and side. They are required to do more running, tackling and heading. They are also there to be tackled. But Bryan also had an above average number of injuries because he always put his body into situations very bravely without having the physical make-up to take it. His head and his heart were always the dominating factors."

It wasn't just in the later stages of his career that Bryan had to dig deep and persevere because like three other players in my Perfect 10 – Denis Law, George Best and Nobby Stiles – he started out as something of a shrimp with not everyone convinced that he would make it as a professional.

He grew up in Chester-le-Street in County Durham and as a schoolboy was invited for trials by a few clubs, but the place that appealed to him the most was West Bromwich Albion after being spotted by Bill Emery, their scout in the North East. He signed for them on schoolboy forms and went to the Midlands for training during the holidays and to play in the occasional match.

He was still on the small side when he reached the age of 15 and the time arrived for deciding whether he was good enough to be taken on as an apprentice. Don Howe, the Albion manager and later an England coach, said: "In those days we were allowed a maximum of 15 apprentices so I asked our chief scout, Reg Ryan, how many we had agreed to take that year. He said 11, so I said, 'well, we've got some space, we'll tell his father we'll give the boy a chance but that we have reservations and are not 100 per cent about him making it.'"

Later Don explained: "He was small but you can sense when a young man has something, and looking at Bryan, I thought he had got character, an inner confidence."

It proved to be a highly perceptive assessment, though it was still some time away before it was there for all to see. Even Bryan had reservations and after a month as an apprentice he phoned the scout who had encouraged him back home, Bill Emery, to say he wasn't happy. It wasn't homesickness, he explained, but simply that he wasn't showing up well against the other youngsters.

"I'm last in all the sprints and shuttles," he told him. Emery spoke to the club and was reassured that though Bryan was frequently last, there was no need to worry because he thought quicker than most of the others. Don Howe confirmed: "Often Bryan would be in a shirt too big for him, but beating the bigger boys and starting to look good. The coaches told me he had this tremendous energy level."

Albion worked on him in training and back at his digs his landlady started every day for him with Guinness, which in those days he hated, but size and strength were not his only problems. The youngster soon had to call on his commitment and tenacity in the face of early injuries that would have turned away many a boy from the idea of a career as a professional footballer.

In season 1976-77 he broke his leg, not once, but three times. The first fracture was playing against Spurs when he was kicked as he made a tackle. Eight weeks later he broke the same leg in the same place playing for the reserves. With typical determination he recovered but just before the end of the season he broke his other leg and was out of action for four months.

Says Bryan: "I lost a year. The worst part was that it happened before I was established. When you are recognised and are injured everyone is waiting for your return, but when you have never been there, you just get forgotten."

It was a huge blow because Robson had hardly had time to make his mark after making his first-team debut under manager Johnny Giles in 1975 away to York City. He fought back, though, with his hallmark tenacity and had Giles saying: "In two years Bryan became a man very quickly. He got physically stronger and his confidence grew."

The arrival of Ron Atkinson as manager of Albion in 1978 saw Bryan confirmed as a player of immense potential and influence. After being capped at youth, U21 and B levels he was given a full England debut against the Republic of Ireland in 1980. It was the start of a brilliant international career that would see him win 90 caps and score 26 goals.

Bryan and Ron Atkinson developed a good rapport, so much so, that after Ron had succeeded Dave Sexton as manager of Manchester United he wasted no time going back to The Hawthorns to sign the player destined to become the heart and soul of Manchester United. Ronnie Allen, who had succeeded Atkinson as manager fought hard to keep the player and even marked him up with a £2m price tag, but the player wanted to move and in the end United paid a record £1.5m for Robson in a £2m package that also included Remi Moses, another gritty midfielder.

Ron Atkinson was desperate to get Robson because as he explained to me at the time: "United have some good players in both defence and attack, but I just don't see who is going to stop the opposition tearing through our midfield." Robson and Moses were the perfect answer though regrettably Moses became dogged by injury. Troubled times with injuries also lay ahead for Robson but he was like the million-dollar man, they always seemed to find a spare part to keep him going.

"I had been at Albion for eight years and felt I needed a change. They didn't seem to think of themselves as a big club. When top players came up for sale you never heard about West Brom making offers. I wanted a big club with big ideas at that point in my career. I wanted to win things which is why I was happy to join Manchester United."

Bryan signed for the Reds out on the pitch before kick-off

against Wolves on October 3, 1981, and then watched as his new team went on to win 5-0 with a hat-trick from Sammy McIlroy, but as Atkinson had pointed out, United were fine going forward and Wolves that day hadn't offered much in attack.

His League debut came in the following game against Manchester City at Maine Road in front of a 52,037 crowd and he played solidly in a goalless game. Robson celebrated his transfer by helping United finish third in his first season and then the following year enjoyed a run to reach two cup finals. He didn't play in the Milk Cup final against Liverpool because of torn ankle ligaments and the Reds went down 2-1 after extra time. The feeling was that if Robson had played, United might well have won.

He did play in the second final and was in the thick of the action against Brighton. The first game ended 2-2 after extra time but they made no mistake in the replay with an emphatic 4-0 victory.

Robson was in one of his uncompromising moods again. He scored the opening goal, and then after Norman Whiteside had put United further ahead, he clinched victory by scoring from Frank Stapleton's header. He even played a part in the fourth goal, winning a penalty as he drove into the area for Arnold Muhren to convert.

Wembley was the kind of place Robson liked to be, and even though the Championship was continuing to be elusive, the team had still finished third in the League. The following season, 1983-84, saw them finish fourth in the table but delighting the fans with a storming run to the semi-finals of the European Cup Winners' Cup. After Bryan had performed his heroics against Barcelona in the quarter-final, United drew Juventus. The first leg at Old Trafford was drawn 1-1 with a goal from Alan Davies but without an injured Robson for the return in Turin the Reds crashed out 2-1 with Whiteside United's scorer.

There was no denying that Robson had given the side something extra and the following year in season 1984-85 they were back at Wembley after knocking out Liverpool in a cracking semi-final replay at Maine Road. In the final they beat Everton 1-0 in extra time following the sending-off of Kevin Moran. Whiteside was the scorer and Robson had picked up his second trophy to justify his transfer.

Season 1985-86 saw United make the kind of start that Robson believed would bring him his dream of a Championship medal. They won their first 10 League games to set a club record, but then things went dramatically wrong for both Robson and his club. The captain tore his hamstring playing for England and aggravated the injury in a comeback game at Sheffield Wednesday. When he finally got back he twisted his ankle and frustration saw him sent off for the first time in his career in a cup tie at Sunderland.

But there was worse to come when he fell heavily at West Ham, dislocating the shoulder he had first damaged the previous season when he had skidded into the advertising hoardings playing against Coventry at Old Trafford. He was in serious trouble now and with the 1986 World Cup in Mexico round the corner, the England manager Bobby Robson wanted the player to have an operation to repair the shoulder. But that would have put him out of action for United and both the player and Ron Atkinson felt there was still a chance of winning the League - provided Robson kept playing of course.

It was a classic clash of club and country. As it turned out United finished fourth again and the player was able to contribute only 21 League appearances in a nightmare season. It looked as if 'Action Man' was beginning to come apart at the seams!

So Bryan went to Mexico with endless speculation about his shoulder which he tried to protect by wearing a special harness that he later abandoned because he said it restricted the balance of his movement. He played against Mexico in a warm-up match and dislocated his shoulder for a third time, and it became a matter of when he would become available, especially after straining his troublesome hamstring in a training game. The debate about his fitness ran on the kind of lines that surrounded Wayne Rooney at the World Cup in Germany 20 years later!

Robson in fact surprised us by declaring himself fit to play against Morocco but he was bowled over and dislocated his shoulder for a fourth time. Although he said he was ready to play against Poland, England wouldn't risk him and he was eventually flown home to have the shoulder pinned and leave the argument raging as to whether that was what should have been done initially! Certainly that's what the England manager would have done as he declared: "With a fit Bryan Robson we would have won the World Cup!" It's a bit of a sweeping claim but there is no doubt that Bobby Robson held the player almost in awe.

Despite the trials and tribulations of the World Cup in Mexico, and Bryan injured in only the second game, the England manager was still trumpeting the merits of 'Captain Marvel' four years later as he prepared for Italia '90. Talking about his skipper after he had scored a couple of goals at Wembley in the run-up to Italy he declared: "He is worth his weight in gold to club and country. He is priceless and a player I couldn't replace.

"For me he is the Player of the Eighties. There has been Peter Shilton, Kevin Keegan and Trevor Brooking but Robson came in at the start of the decade and he is still playing like a man inspired. There is simply not another midfield player like him – and I mean anywhere in the world. He is not just a captain and inspiration to the team, he is a match-winner. You name me another who can do what this man has done for us for so long.

"The Mexico World Cup was one of the biggest disappointments of my career and it was because the skipper was injured. Don't forget we got to the quarter-finals without him. With him we would have gone all the way.

"If anyone deserves to win something now it is Bryan. I hope he gets lucky and this turns out to be the greatest season of his life. It would be a reward for a great player. He should be able to sit back in retirement and look at a cupboard full of cups and medals. Lesser players have won more but none has given as much.

"You are not taught to play like Bryan Robson, it is in-born. It is in-built determination that separates the men from the boys. The wonderful thing for England is that he is playing better than ever. When I select a squad I always hope there are no dropouts and the last man you want to drop out is the skipper. If he tells you he is injured your heart sinks. You ask yourself: 'Who is there to replace him?' And the answer is no-one."

As England prepared for the World Cup in Italy, Ron Atkinson, now manager of Sheffield Wednesday after being sacked by United to make way for Alex Ferguson, also chipped in with a tribute and said it was a crying shame that Bryan Robson had never been voted Footballer of the Year.

"He is light years in front of the other contenders because of what he has done. It is World Cup year and he has carried his country there on his back. When I signed Bryan he was a great player and he still is. It is difficult to pay him a bigger compliment than to say neither his club nor country can do without him," he said.

"He is a schoolboy's dream to watch and any youngster should use him as a yardstick for their ambitions. He is an idol and a hero simply by the way he plays. When you watch Bryan Robson you can't fail to be inspired and proud."

With these tributes around, hopes were high and expectations soaring but Bryan's injury jinx struck again. Once again in only the second match of the tournament he tore the

Achilles tendon on his left leg while he was simply running, no tackle or anything like that. He pulled up in agony and that was Bryan's World Cup over, and like Mexico, before it had really started.

This time he was spirited out of Sardinia and flown home for an immediate operation in the hope that at least he would be ready for United's next season after the low point of finishing 13th in the table with Fergie still signing players and desperately trying to fit them into a balanced side.

In fact the operation saw him miss the start of season 1990-91 for United and it was the beginning of the end for his international career. Bryan and new England manager Graham Taylor had a bumpy ride until he retired following a European Championship qualifying tie against Turkey in the October. The match was won 1-0 but he announced his retirement the following month with the proud record of 90 caps, 65 of them as captain, and 26 goals to his name.

His target had been a hundred caps but he was being played out of position with England and at the age of 34 he thought it was time to concentrate on United.

He had played in three World Cups, but two of them were ruined for him by his injuries, and as Bobby Robson says, England were never the same without him. Nevertheless he can look back on more than a few international high spots, like his hat-trick in an 8-0 win against Turkey, and I remember watching with pleasure when he startled us all by scoring against Yugoslavia after just 38 seconds, the fastest goal Wembley had ever seen.

Back at Old Trafford, Alex Ferguson was ready to launch into orbit. He had started by winning the FA Cup in 1990 and the European Cup Winners' Cup the following season with Robson making four appearances including a role in the final against Barcelona in Rotterdam.

He was a regular the following season when the League Cup

was secured (although United were pipped to the title by Leeds United) but in season 1992-93 when United won the Championship after 26 years without it, he wasn't the regular he had been and the substitutes' bench was his starting point over the last few crucial weeks. Eric Cantona was now the main man and it was Steve Bruce wearing the captain's armband to leave Bryan as the club captain.

Bryan Robson had played in the wrong era in terms of winning the League on a regular basis in keeping with his great talent, and he only just made it, making 14 appearances, including one replacing Lee Sharpe to share in the 3-1 victory against Blackburn Rovers at Old Trafford that finally won them the Championship.

Steve Bruce and Bryan Robson went up together for the presentation and as the pair of them held up the trophy in the directors' box there was as much relief that Robson had finally made it as there was joy in seeing the Championship return to Old Trafford after its long absence.

Robson recalled at the time: "I remember 17 years ago being top of the League when I was at West Bromwich, only to be overtaken by Liverpool. We finished fourth. I have wanted a Championship medal since that moment. At times I thought it would never happen!"

There was one more game to play that season, a return to Selhurst Park for a 2-1 win over Wimbledon. Paul Ince got the opening goal and fittingly it was Bryan Robson, on from the start in this match, who scored his first of the season and the last of the campaign.

During the summer Alex Ferguson signed Roy Keane to put even more pressure on Bryan Robson. He started the season in the team, and indeed scored on the opening day against Norwich in a 2-0 win. He played in the last game of the season, too, for a total of 10 League starts and five appearances as a substitute. For the most part, though, he had become a bit-part player as the Reds won the Championship again and went on to beat Chelsea 4-0 to complete the Double.

The real blow, though, came when Ferguson couldn't even find a place for his 37-year-old stalwart on the bench at Wembley, because as he explained he had to look to younger players who would be with him the next season.

Robson said: "The disappointment for me was that having played an important role to get us to the final I felt I deserved to be involved. A place on the bench would have been a fair compromise, but then that's my biased take on it. I found it a little strange and uncomfortable at Wembley because I was with the squad, wearing my club suit on the sidelines, so close to the action.

"The fans helped me. They were brilliant. They appreciated what I had done over 13 years at the club. They chanted my name and made me feel a lot better.

"But it was time to move on and, despite my disappointment over the 1994 FA Cup final, I could look back on a fantastic career with United. I had three winners' medals in the FA Cup, two in the Championship and one in the European Cup Winners' Cup. I played my part in taking the club back to the top of the English game, where they would remain for many more years."

So, indeed, it was time to move on and that close season Bryan Robson moved to become player-manager of Middlesbrough, as well as taking up an appointment as assistant to new England manager Terry Venables.

He took Middlesbrough to promotion to the Premiership in his first season, and though they went back down two years later, he brought them back up and in his seven years took 'Boro to three cup finals. Bryan then managed Bradford City and West Bromwich Albion, but was out of work for eight months until May of this year when he was appointed manager of Sheffield United following the dismissal of Neil Warnock.

While he was on the sidelines I could not understand why the

FA did not give him the England U21 manager's job when Sven Goran Eriksson was sacked and Stuart Pearce, under-performing as manager of Manchester City, was brought in for the junior post on a part-time basis. The City board didn't want Pearce to take the job and the appointment certainly wasn't popular with the fans, who thought their manager would have been better served concentrating on the Blues without distractions.

Robson, on the other hand, was unemployed and so rich in international experience as both a player and as an assistant to Terry Venables. He would have been perfect, but then the FA's track record with their international appointments has never been their strong point. For me, the fact that they ignored Robson was a horrendous oversight. I believe England's loss will prove to be Sheffield United's gain.

As Sir Alex Ferguson wrote for a Football Association Writers tribute evening to Bryan and his wife Denise in 2006 when Robson was still manager of West Bromwich Albion: "When I arrived at Manchester United in November 1986, I was lucky enough to inherit the best captain I have ever had in terms of inspiration and respect in the dressing room. I have been fortunate to work with a lot of great players but Bryan was up there with the best. He was incredible, a fantastic player. His endurance was amazing, as he proved by coming back time and time again from serious injuries, including three broken legs and shoulder and Achilles injuries.

"Now he is a fellow Barclays Premiership manager and while I'm absolutely delighted about that, I am not surprised. It's not easy to predict which of your players will make successful managers. Those you think are cut out for it don't always make the transition while others you never thought had it in them surprise you. But Bryan was a certainty to become a boss because he was always a decision maker as a player and absolutely spot-on tactically on the pitch, too.

"Switching from playing to management is a big step. Bryan left Old Trafford as a player one day and the next he was manager of Middlesbrough. That was a great learning curve for him. Now West Brom are capitalising and benefiting from the experience he gained in his first managerial position. It's great to see him back in business and being honoured tonight."

My postscript is to say it would have been even greater had the Football Association had the sense and loyalty to make him the manager of the England U21 team!

BRYAN ROBSON - CAREER STATS

BORN:	Chester-le-Street
DATE OF BIRTH:	January 11 1957
JOINED UNITED:	October 1981
UNITED LEAGUE APPS:	345
GOALS:	74
INT. CAPS (England):	90
GOALS:	26

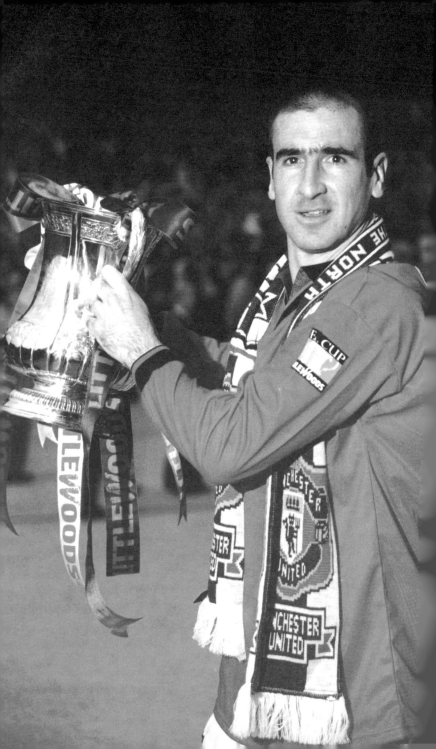

1992-1997
Eric
Cantona

Eric Cantona seemed to come from nowhere and four-and-a-half years later, he disappeared just as abruptly. But what is certain is that the Frenchman changed the course of history for Manchester United.

In terms of the League Championship, United had been going nowhere since the days of Sir Matt Busby. It had been 26 years since they had won the First Division and there had been a succession of managers who had tried and failed to maintain the success that Busby had brought to the club.

Wilf McGuinness, Frank O'Farrell, Tommy Docherty, Dave Sexton and Ron Atkinson had all had their moments of glory in Cup football but had never been able to get a team playing with the consistency required to win a League competition.

Then Alex Ferguson arrived from Aberdeen to change all that and has since proved himself a phenomenal manager, with nine Championships in his 21-year managerial reign, but he would be the first to concede that the big break-through for his success came when he signed Eric Cantona from Leeds United.

Ferguson had bought extensively but had been finding it difficult to blend his new players into a team, so much so that season 1989-90 saw his misfits heading for the relegation area and in fact finishing the season in 13th place. Winning the FA Cup that same season saved the day for him and bought him time, which he made good use of by winning the European Cup

Winners' Cup the following year. The League remained a different matter, even though they did manage an improvement to finish in fifth place. The following year saw them runners-up to Leeds but the real turning point in their Championship fortunes came the moment the maverick Cantona walked through the door from Elland Road for a bargain-basement fee of £1.2m in November 1992.

The transfer happened almost by accident as a result of Bill Fotherby, the Leeds managing director, phoning United chairman Martin Edwards to see if their former player, Denis Irwin, could be bought. Ferguson was with Edwards at the time and the inquiry was promptly turned down, but with the manager prompting his chairman to ask about the availability of Cantona, to their great surprise they received an encouraging response.

Why did Leeds decide to move Cantona on after he had played a big part in their Championship success the previous season?

I suspect that Cantona did not fit easily into how manager Howard Wilkinson perceived footballers, and a few years later I asked him why he thought Cantona had been such a big success at Old Trafford after moving him out of Elland Road. He told me that it was like sowing seeds and that it depended on the ground as to whether they failed or flourished, and I guess what he was trying to tell me was that Manchester United were able to provide a much more fertile soil for Cantona than he had found at Elland Road. It sounded as if Howard had been talking philosophy with Cantona.

Perhaps, though, Howard never felt as confident as Ferguson of being able to handle a man whose disciplinary track record in France had left a lot to be desired. In fact Eric had been a professional for nearly nine years and his career had gone nowhere really significant except to achieve notoriety as the "enfant terrible" of French football. He had virtually had to flee his own country in order to find a club willing to take him on and even in England it had proved difficult. It hadn't worked out at Sheffield Wednesday where he had a brief trial and despite helping Leeds United win the Championship, I suspect he and Howard Wilkinson had had a bumpy ride.

Ferguson said: "I see Eric as a Manchester United player, the kind we want at this club. He has style, he has class, and this club will suit him. His goalscoring was instrumental in the success of Leeds last year. I am happy to bring another striker to the club, one who has a good reputation and one who won't in any way be overawed at playing at Old Trafford." It didn't take long for everyone to appreciate that the manager was right and that Eric Cantona was finally in the right place at the right time and working for the right manager.

The new signing watched his new team-mates beat Arsenal at Highbury before making his debut as a substitute the following week against Manchester City at Old Trafford to share in a 2-1 win. His full debut came in the next match with a 1-0 home win against leaders Norwich on December 12 to see United move into third place.

United continued unbeaten into the New Year, including a dramatic 3-3 draw at Sheffield Wednesday after trailing 3-0. It was Cantona who got the equaliser, an early demonstration of his ability to score important goals.

The Cantona-inspired Reds began weighing in with some big scores too, such as 5-0 against Coventry, 4-1 against Spurs, until finally they beat Liverpool 2-1 at Anfield to go top of the table. A defeat and a run of three draws saw them slip back to third but they went back into the lead by beating the leaders 3-1 at Norwich with Cantona among the scorers. A winning run took them to the Championship 10 points ahead of Aston Villa and Cantona's place in United folklore was secure.

The chant of "oo-aah-Cantona" has regularly rung round Old Trafford ever since. The fans will never forget him. They will remember his more troubled times as well of course, such as his kung-fu attack on a Crystal Palace supporter that would come a little later in his United career, but nothing then or since will sully the romance rooted in the long awaited Championship of 1993.

Last season marked the 10th anniversary of Cantona's retirement from football and so powerful is his legacy, back home in France as well as around Manchester, that the French sports paper *L'Equipe* devoted an entire issue to a player who had to leave his own country to fulfil himself in football.

Writer Erik Bielderman went to great lengths to find and interview the people who were caught in the photograph of the kung-fu incident at Selhurst Park and discover that they have all been left with warm memories of an incident that scandalised the nation at the time.

Erik also set out to re-enact Cantona's iconic style of wearing his collar turned up by photographing Sir Alex Ferguson not only wearing his collar turned up, but wearing the same haughty, superior look that was so much part of the Cantona persona. The United manager does not lend himself easily to media stunts, but because it was a salute to one of his favourite players, he happily posed a là Cantona.

He was not the only one pleased to join in the tribute to the Frenchman. Eric's father, Albert, mother Eleonore, along with his two brothers, Jean-Marie and Joel, are all photographed with upturned collars. That's perhaps something you might expect from family, but also staring out of the pages of *L'Equipe Magazine* in similar poses are Eric's former manager at Auxerre, Guy Roux, along with goalkeeper Fabien Barthez and United players of today, Cristiano Ronaldo and Ryan Giggs. None of course was able to capture totally the Cantona look because it wasn't just his upturned collar but his straight back, chest stuck out and the arrogant stare of his eyes.

Nike got nearer to capturing the look in that memorable advert that appeared on big billboards when the European Championships were played in England, saying: "1966 was a good year for English football" and everybody immediately thinks of England's World Cup victory, only to be pulled up short by the next line: "Eric was born."

Eric has appeared in some equally striking photographs that have had him dressed up in all manner of costumes, behind the bars of a confessional box, and nude down to the hips in a picture called *L'Artiste*.

But of course, it is as a god who came down from on high to lead their team out of the wilderness and into the long promised land of the Championship that will remain most vividly in the minds of United fans. That and the fact that he was a key factor in going on to help the Reds win a total of four Premiership titles and two FA Cups in his four-and-a-half years at Old Trafford.

It's got to be said that the supporters will never forget either the sensational attack on Matthew Simmons in the game against Crystal Palace on January 25, 1995, at Selhurst Park. The incident was triggered initially by Richard Shaw pulling Cantona back by the shirt. The irritated Frenchman turned on his opponent and kicked him for which he was promptly sent off by referee Alan Wilkie.

Cantona headed for the dressing rooms with the home crowd inevitably jeering and booing as Simmons rushed to the barrier to hurl more personal abuse. Eric hesitated, walked on but then obviously changed his mind and leaped over the fence to go feet first at the man baiting him. Kit man Norman Davies had set off as escort to guide Eric to the dressing room but he could only watch helplessly as Eric disappeared into the crowd. Paul Ince, always close to Eric as a pal, rushed to the incident and was later himself charged with assault, though he was found not guilty when his case was heard at the end of the season.

Cantona, meanwhile, with Peter Schmeichel also now on

hand, was ushered off the pitch to the safety of the dressing room. He went back to Manchester with the rest of the team that night, but later had to return to Croydon Magistrates Court to answer a charge of assault.

Meanwhile, the media was in overdrive with the picture of his kung-fu kick going round the world. Some wanted him thrown out of the country and never allowed to play football in England again. There were even calls for him to be given a life ban. It was knockabout hysterical stuff, and I am happy to say that I went for a more balanced view in the *Manchester Evening News*. I called for an immediate ban, which is what happened, and Manchester United also kept a sense of proportion. The club said they were suspending him until the end of the season and fined him the maximum allowed of two weeks wages.

United felt that their instant and quite harsh punishment would be enough to satisfy the FA disciplinary commission that was set up to deal with Cantona and they were shocked when the three-man panel extended his suspension until the end of September, which of course took him into the following season, missing the first 10 games or so. They also fined him a further £10,000.

But there was worse to come when his case was heard at Croydon Magistrates Court where the chairman, Mrs Jean Pearch, stunned everyone by sentencing the player to two months imprisonment. United immediately appealed and at Croydon Crown Court the following week the judge acknowledged that Simmons had indulged in action that would have "provoked the most stoic." The jail sentence was quashed and instead Eric was ordered to serve 120 hours of community service, something incidentally that he undertook very conscientiously coaching 10-year-old youngsters from Salford Schools for four hours a day at The Cliff training ground.

Eric, being Eric, still managed to have the last word, appearing at a Press conference after the court appeal, to mystify everyone with his now famous quote: "When the seagulls follow the trawler, it's because they think sardines will be thrown into the sea."

It could be a reference to the Press following the good ship Cantona in the expectation of quotes and pictures, or it could have been just another flight of the Frenchman's philosophy. He did once admit to me when I asked him about some of his more bizarre quotes that he sometimes said what he thought people wanted to hear!

The outcome for United was that without Cantona they finished the season in second place, a point behind Blackburn, even though they did beat Ipswich 9-0.

Even Alex Ferguson at first felt that it would be impossible for Cantona to continue his career at United. He worried about the hostility Cantona would face at away grounds, but gradually he came round to thinking that if the player was prepared to give it a go, he would back him.

How does Eric remember those tumultuous days? Did he feel guilty after karate-kicking the fan?

Ten years on, he tells *L'Equipe's* Jean-Philippe Leclaire: "The next morning I did not really analyse the situation. I did not know what happened or what was going to happen. I was not really aware of things. Of course I was not proud of myself. We are just men with a fragile side. It does not matter if a man suffers. It does not matter if a man cries. That highly-strung sensibility might enable you to move mountains later.

"When that hooligan called me "a French son of a bitch" I had heard it 50 billion times before. However, on that day I did not react as I used to. Why? I never found any answer to that."

So Ferguson took a gamble on his wayward star. There was talk of a transfer to Inter Milan, but just before the end of the season he signed a new three-year contract to play on at Old Trafford.

He announced at the time: "It is a love story. It is something that is very strong for me. The love of the club is the most important weapon in the world. I just couldn't leave. It is something very strong for me."

But Cantona was not the only issue demanding the attention of the manager. Ferguson was reshaping his squad and he shocked a great many fans when he dispensed with three highly popular players in the form of Paul Ince, Mark Hughes and Andrei Kanchelskis. The reason was that he was looking to the class of '92 who had won the FA Youth Cup, and he felt that they were ready now to take on more responsibility and that they would continue to blossom and improve under the tutelage of Eric Cantona. Alan Hansen came out with his infamous clanger: "You will never win anything with kids", but the United manager knew what he was doing and kept faith with his new French leader.

Eric returned to action for the home game against Liverpool on October 1. Nicky Butt scored first but two goals by Robbie Fowler saw United trailing 2-1. Then into the picture strode Cantona. Ryan Giggs was pulled down and Eric, shrugging off the pressure that had marked his return, coolly converted the spot-kick to level at 2-2 and earn his team a valuable point. The Frenchman continued to show the way and finished the season as top scorer on 14 goals, despite starting the season late because of his ban. The Reds fell behind with Newcastle 12 points ahead at one stage but a storming run over the last few weeks saw them leapfrog the one-time leaders to win the Championship four points ahead of the Geordies.

They won the League the following season as well. The gamble of keeping Cantona had paid off big time, though I do believe Eric owes Manchester United every bit as much as the club and its supporters owe to him.

Cantona had been the luckiest man in creation to land at United when he did to work for Ferguson at the start of a new era featuring some highly talented youngsters. Once at Old

Trafford his career changed almost overnight. Everything fell into place and Cantona found a manager who understood him, and was prepared to make allowances for some of his eccentric dress habits. He must also have counted his blessings when Fergie started to introduce a bunch of highly talented youngsters who were full of running and prepared to give him the adoration that must have been manna from heaven for a professional of no little ego.

Above all he could not fail to realise that the club was a success waiting to happen and needing just one final piece of the jigsaw to create a truly marvellous picture.

One of football's favourite theories is that new players, especially foreign ones, need time to settle in, but Cantona instantly transformed the team, changing them from challengers to champions. He arrived in the November, scored four goals in his first five games and proceeded to strike a wonderful rapport with players like Mark Hughes, Paul Ince, Ryan Giggs and Lee Sharpe.

And so it continued as youngsters were brought in to play acolyte to the man's godlike presence. The kung-fu incident threatened to blow the whole thing sky high, and that's when the player really had cause to be grateful to club and manager. Ferguson's decision to support him was the moment when Cantona should have counted his lucky stars. It was a remarkable act of faith by Ferguson in face of the hysterical clamour at a time when the mood around the country was that he should follow in the footsteps of an even more famous countryman into exile in Elba.

Cantona stayed to share in two more Championships involving a second League and Cup double, a fantastic achievement which ensured his place among the Old Trafford legends.

The fans certainly enjoyed 'The Double' season of 1995-96 because winning the FA Cup involved beating the old enemy from Liverpool – and Cantona was the hero as the scorer of the goal in a 1-0 win just five minutes from the end as the prospect of extra time loomed. David James had punched David Beckham's corner-kick well out of his penalty area, only for Cantona to meet it on the volley and smash it back the way it had come for a marvellously scored goal.

As Ferguson said afterwards: "It was a quite magnificent goal. Eric showed great composure and such accuracy with the shot. It couldn't have come at a better time. Eric Cantona makes the difference. Even when he has a quiet day as he did in this match there is always something left in the tank. I don't know many players who could have hit the ball the way he did. What an impact. He won the Cup for us."

The kung-fu moment had been forgotten and forgiven, certainly by United supporters and even wider afield with the Football Writers' Association voting him their Player of the Year. He scored a total of 19 goals that season and said: "Winning the double was important after what had happened. I have the highest regard for Alex Ferguson as a man and as a manager. What can I say about the fans? I respect them and I love them and I try to give them the pleasure they need to receive. While I was banned they remembered me during every game even if it was just for 15 seconds. I will never forget that."

Cantona captained United to their third successive Championship the following year, finishing seven points in front of Newcastle this time. Cantona weighed in with 11 League goals but a week after the skipper had been presented with the Premiership trophy on May 18, United called a Press conference to announce that Eric Cantona was retiring from football with immediate effect.

Martin Edwards said in a prepared statement: "I am extremely sorry Eric has arrived at this decision, but understand and respect his reasons. Many of us believe Eric has been the catalyst for the most successful period in our history. It has truly been a magical time."

Alex Ferguson said: "Eric has had a huge impact on the development of our younger players. He has been a model professional in the way he conducted himself and a joy to manage. He is certainly one of the most gifted and dedicated players I have had the pleasure of working with. He leaves with our best wishes and will always be welcome at Old Trafford. He has given us so many wonderful memories."

Then Eric wound up his playing career in a statement that read: "I have played professional football for 13 years, which is a long time. I always planned to retire when I was at the top and at Manchester United I have reached the pinnacle of my career. In the last four-and-a-half years I have enjoyed my best football and had a wonderful time. I have had a marvellous relationship with the manager, coach, staff and players and not least the fans. I wish Manchester United even more success in the future."

Eric was now departing as quickly as he had arrived and with hindsight it was probably a good time to go, even though we were all puzzled as to why he had chosen that particular moment. Maybe it was because in the final few weeks of the season he had become simply another player rather than an inspiration, and that was a situation that I don't think would have appealed to this proud Frenchman.

At the outset, the pairing of Eric Cantona and Alex Ferguson had looked to many people like an accident waiting to happen. It seemed inevitable that sooner or later there would be an almighty collision of wills. It had looked the ultimate clash of nit-picking disciplinarian and rebel free spirit. Yet somehow Ferguson, he who dishes out the hairdryer treatment, managed to get more out of the player than any of his other managers, and they established a good working relationship.

Cups and saucers have flown in Ferguson's dressing rooms for offences, which in comparison with Cantona's embarrassing behaviour, were kindergarten stuff. Yet the volatile Frenchman stayed the course to become a trawler in calm waters.

The truth of the matter of course is that in footballing terms Alex Ferguson was in love with Eric Cantona and we all know that at times love can be quite blind. But this was not a blindness born of ignorance, because Ferguson knows genius when he sees it and he certainly discerned it in his flamboyant Frenchman. The United manager will tell you that happiness could be simply looking out of his office window at The Cliff training ground watching the man train, so marvellously did he move and work the ball.

Cantona was not just their leading scorer, he brought out more from those around him and most importantly, time and again break open a seemingly deadlocked match. He could unpick a defence to create an opening.

So highly did he rate him that Ferguson virtually tore up the rulebook for the Frenchman, something which 'Sergeant Wilko' at Leeds had not been prepared to do. But ever the realist, Ferguson knew what he was doing because in day-to-day life Cantona was an impeccable professional. He might have had to flee France and come to England because there was nowhere else for him to go in football, but in training he is a role model. After a normal stint Cantona was the one who stayed out to practise his ball skills and tricks. He was frequently the last away from the training ground because he used to sign more autograph books than anyone else.

His problem of course was his temper, the volatile streak always lurking close to the surface that saw him explode uncontrollably when provoked. Cantona retaliates on a massive scale, as the world saw only too well in the fateful match against Crystal Palace. But Ferguson understood him. They shared a similar low tolerance level. A Fergie tongue-lashing can blister paint as any number of footballers and journalists can tell you but there was one particular moment in their relationship when he and Cantona reached absolute rapport and which I believe cemented a bond that saw them survive as a partnership.

The United manager explained: "I was stressing to Eric the need to control himself or he would lose everything. At the same time I told him I knew what it was like because as a player myself I was sent off five or six times in my career.

"As soon as I told him that he smiled and I think he looked at me in a new light as someone who had been through a similar battle with temperament, a kindred spirit in fact, and we understood one another better.

"I don't believe there is anything wrong in losing your temper, provided it is for the right reasons. If you have passion and commitment it is only a short step. I don't excuse Eric for kicking the man at Selhurst Park who was abusing him, or for his other excesses, but I do understand and I have no regrets about bringing him to Old Trafford."

Eric won a special place in the hearts of Manchester United supporters during his time in England and he will remain in their eyes for evermore the god who came down from on high to lead their team to the promised land of the Championship. The fans loved him – and still do – because until he arrived at Old Trafford they had endured 26 long, frustrating years without winning the League. Then as soon as he started playing, despite arriving midway through a season, the United team was transformed.

Alex Ferguson had found the perfect foil for his young players as well as injecting into his team a striker who could change the course of a game on his own with a touch of magic and a goal. One season when the team lost its form around Christmas, the Frenchman virtually single-handed carried the rest of the players on his back by repeatedly scoring match-winning goals, and they won the League.

The arrogant strut and familiar turned-up collar that always

ERIC CANTONA

marked him out as someone different and special will never be forgotten in Manchester. Nor will his beautiful football, the telling pass, the vision, the masterly goals and all the other superb touches that contributed so much to the four Premiership titles and two FA Cup wins United enjoyed during his spell at Old Trafford.

It's true his powers had waned slightly towards the end. He hadn't been quite so influential in his last season, even though as captain he had led the team to yet another championship. He had become simply a player rather than an inspiration and many were disappointed that he wasn't able to conjure up something special to have turned the two games against Borussia Dortmund in the semi-final of the European Champions League. Each tie was lost narrowly 1-0 and United missed many chances, including one opportunity by Cantona that a year before he would have buried without blinking.

Cantona was 31 when he left Manchester to retire completely from all football, but some fans still insisted on forming a group dedicated to bringing the Frenchman back to Old Trafford. They failed to persuade him to change his mind, but it was an indication of the love and loyalty he had inspired.

People wondered if there would be life for United after Cantona but he had done his job well. The young players who respected and looked up to him were ready to spread their wings and fly without the help of their French mentor. Gary Neville, David Beckham, Nicky Butt, Ryan Giggs, Phil Neville and Paul Scholes had come of age and were ready to stand on their own feet. Cantona had helped them to develop, a legacy to his great contribution to United history. The Frenchman's spirit lived on with the young players he taught so much, and Eric Cantona was warmly remembered when Manchester United clinched their treble and conquered Europe in 1999.

Sir Alex Ferguson simply says: "Eric graced our stage splendidly. It was a pleasure just to watch him training and he undoubtedly raised the awareness of our young players at the time. Old Trafford was his spiritual home for nearly five years. He was blessed with a special talent and I was delighted when he came back to play in the Munich Memorial match at Old Trafford to say a proper farewell to his adoring fans."

I helped to organise the match between United and a Cantona XI along with John Doherty, chairman of the Manchester United Former Players' Association and Gordon Taylor, chief executive of the Professional Footballers' Association, and nearly £1m was raised for the survivors and dependants of the Munich air crash. It was a worthy charity, but the highlight for many people was to see Eric Cantona back at Old Trafford and able to say a proper farewell to his fans.

Not that everything was sweetness and light in the Frenchman's relationship with Manchester United at the end. Away from the football, Eric had an issue with the club's commercial activities which he considered had exploited him, and which may also have been a factor in his sudden departure.

Supporters might have been puzzled, for instance, by the disappearance of Cantona shirts and other memorabilia very quickly after his return to France, but as he explains to *L'Equipe*: "Manchester was a lot about merchandising. Sometimes they need you to do a tape, give interviews, write books, take pictures. To avoid my image and name being used all over the place, I signed precise contracts with the club. I gave them the exclusivity on my pictures. However, they did not respect it. I went to see Alex Ferguson, then the chairman, Martin Edwards, to talk about it. I told them beware, things are happening.

"One morning before a game, on my way to eat breakfast, I saw myself on the front page of a paper. Some people do not care being on a tabloid's front page. They are even proud of it. Well, it destroys me, even if I am on my way to play, it becomes more important than the game.

"I see it as treason. So on the day I said I was quitting I told the club: 'OK I quit, but you should know that I am still suing the merchandising.' I went to court and I won. I did not want to become a product. I asked them to take everything away. And it is gone now."

His quarrel with the club over the commercial activities was only one aspect of his retirement. His last game was against West Ham on May 11, 1997, and he says that when he left the field at the end of the match he felt nothing. "I felt nothing because I wanted to quit. I had had enough. I did not have the flame any more. Football was my life, my childhood passion. When the flame disappears, why continue? To go to the Middle East for 300 billion Euros? I was not interested. I wanted to become an actor. Ten years later it makes me proud to be able to do films."

Life for Eric after Manchester United centred on living in Barcelona for a period and then Paris. He has been involved in several films and on the sporting front has become big in beach football as first captain and then manager of a French national team. He is also now divorced from the wife who was with him in Manchester where he lived in a modest suburban house in contrast to the palatial piles of some of his team-mates.

Eric Cantona was always different and says now: "I don't think I have changed a lot. I would still be able to jump on a guy in the stand. I still occasionally blow a fuse, even if I have learnt to know myself better with time. My ultimate goal is to be totally Zen. I have always wanted that."

So how does Eric want people to remember him? What would he want people to say about Eric Cantona the footballer in 50 years?

He says: "I lived football as it is supposed to be lived. Like a game you have to play honestly. The first thing is to work hard, without losing the notion of pleasure. I hope that is what people will retain from me. With my dark side as well. Maradona, Best lived for and by football. The day they retired they had nothing but their memories. I have the chance to express myself somewhere else. I have other passions, other interests. I do not only live in the memory of what I have been."

ERIC CANTONA - CAREER STATS

BORN:	Paris
DATE OF BIRTH:	May 24 1966
JOINED UNITED:	November 1992
UNITED LEAGUE APPS:	143
GOALS:	64
INT. CAPS (France):	45
GOALS:	20

1990-

Ryan
Giggs

From bright-eyed youngster leading the charge of the class of '92 into the first team, to senior citizen with more honours than any other Manchester United player in the club's history.

That's the remarkable story of Ryan Giggs and the 17 years he has spent at Old Trafford pursuing a career that has brought him 16 major honours involving nine Championships, four FA Cup winners' medals, two League Cup winners' medals and a UEFA Champions League trophy.

What is perhaps even more remarkable is that he remains completely unspoilt with the same enthusiasm for the game that marked him out when he became the first member of the talented team that won the FA Youth Cup in 1992 to break into the senior side.

It was the manner of the boy as much as his great talent that first caught my attention. It's the eyes which strike you, dark and unwavering, they gaze unflinchingly straight at you suggesting an honesty that has seen him through some testing times to become one of the most respected players in the game.

Ryan has made more than 700 appearances in senior competitions for United and it could well be that before he has completed his career he will match the record 759 games played for the Reds by Sir Bobby Charlton. Already he stands shoulder to shoulder with the legendary Charlton as a player who has always represented the finer things of football. As Sir Alex Ferguson once put it to me: "Ryan Giggs has led his life well, both on and off the field.

"You never hear anything untoward about him and it cannot always have been easy for him in his younger days when, with his outstanding and exciting ability allied to his good looks, he was forced to walk the celebrity road.

"I tried to protect him from the glare of publicity at first because he was so young when he first came into prominence. But he was also clever enough to shun most of the hype himself, a wise decision which I think suited his personality and allowed him to develop his game to the point where he can perform successfully against the best in the world.

"He is a calm person with a natural composure, which balanced with his passion to play, gives him an ideal temperament capable of handling the pressure of playing at the highest of levels.

"He is our longest-serving player now and has won everything, yet his enthusiasm and ambition are undiminished.

"I use him as a role model for young players coming into the club. I am proud to think I may have helped in his development. In fact any father would be proud to have a son like Ryan Giggs.

"He has been one of the game's best players for over a decade with an exceptional level of consistency and skill. Nobody could underestimate for one minute Ryan's contribution to our successes. He has been central to everything we have achieved and hopefully he will continue to help us to stay at the top.

"To say he is a great professional would be grossly understating the way he conducts his life and career. He has always done things in an impeccable manner and I cannot remember him causing me a single moment's anxiety.

"He is one of the greatest individuals ever to wear the famous red shirt of Manchester United, but that has never stopped him from being totally unselfish and committed in pursuance of the team's ambitions and priorities. Ryan is one of the most gifted players in United's history and the club was fortunate to unearth a player of his calibre.

"He has scored many memorable goals, but it's not just the glittering and outstanding moments of magic that make Ryan such a wonderful and special footballer. There is so much more to his game than just the scoring of the occasional match-winning goal. He is a marvellous all-round player with a depth of ability that is capable of putting the world's greatest defences on the back foot. How many times have we seen defenders scrambling to cover after the ball has arrived at Ryan's feet?

"Watching Ryan blaze down the wing with opposition players trailing in his wake is one of the finest sights in football. Is it any wonder that he has always been considered one of Old Trafford's favourite sons?

"He is without doubt one of Manchester United's all-time greats."

Team-mate Gary Neville is another admirer and says: "The sharpness of his movement is something you cannot appreciate unless you have played against him. I know how good he is because I have to play against him in training every week. If he runs at you and takes you on, you cannot get near him. To me he is the best left winger in the world. Giggsy has just got everything. He is brave, elusive, quick and he works hard.

"He has got a different level of stamina, like David Beckham, from everyone else at the club. I am the type of person who always likes to be at the front in training runs just for my self-confidence but if Giggsy decides he wants to go full out, he just breezes past you. It is almost like he is taking the mickey."

Although Ryan is essentially Mr Nice Guy, to get to the top in football and, what's more, stay there for such a long time, requires a hard core of steel and determination, qualities Ryan showed from quite an early age.

For instance, he is the son of Danny Wilson, a top-class Rugby League player, but when his parents' marriage broke up Ryan was strong-minded enough to change his surname to that of his mother, Lynne Giggs. It was as Ryan Wilson that he first appeared in schoolboy teams, only becoming Ryan Giggs after signing for United to throw all the reporters into confusion.

It was his father's transfer from Cardiff to Swinton Rugby League Club when he was seven years old that brought him to Manchester. He was very much a Welshman and spoke with a Welsh accent until he managed to get rid of it to avoid the inevitable teasing. It seemed his transition from Welsh to Englishman was complete when he was picked for the England international schoolboy team and made captain.

But Giggs insists: "I am a Welshman, and proud of it, but when I was quite young my family moved to the Manchester area and so naturally I went to school there. Playing for my school, Moorside, qualified me to play for the area teams and then on to the international side. It's all quite logical really. If you play for an English school it's a natural step to go on to play for the country of that school. It was only later that I elected to play for Wales as the country of my birth. Before that, I was proud to captain the England Schools team. I played nine times in all. We won seven of them and just lost to Germany and Scotland."

Ryan first signed for United in February 1988, thanks to the alertness of Harold Wood, a United steward who manned the dressing rooms at The Cliff training ground. Explains Ryan: "Out of school I played for a local junior team called Deans in a Sunday League and Harold Wood must have been impressed because he told Sir Alex Ferguson there was a boy he should have a look at playing near where he lived. The manager set the scouting wheels in motion and they invited me to join them. I was in fact going for coaching at that time to Manchester City but that was because our manager at Deans was a City scout and he had three or four of us on City's books. I didn't have to think twice though when the United invitation came because I had always been a United fan. It was a dream!"

It wasn't long before the players were aware of the new arrival, as Ryan recalls: "One of my first training sessions with the senior squad brought me up against Viv Anderson. I was about 14 or 15 at the time and it was a practice match against the first team. I was on the left wing and Viv was marking me. I think he thought he was in for an easy morning and he said he hoped I had had a good breakfast. I got the impression that that was going to be the only good thing likely to happen for me that morning. Anyway, after I had skipped past him a few times, I wouldn't say he lost his temper, but it looked to me like he was beginning to!"

Giggs made his first-team debut as a substitute against Everton but two months later on May 4, 1991, just before the end of the season, he made a full debut against Manchester City and marked it by scoring the only goal of the game in a 1-0 win.

He says: "I couldn't forget that goal because although it is down in the record books as mine I have got to admit that I didn't actually score it! It was an own goal by Colin Hendry, the Manchester City centre-half. I made a run across him and I think it put him off. It looked as if I had scored but he was the last to touch it because I didn't. After the game the Press said they thought I had got a touch. He said he certainly didn't want the goal and I could have it. So it went down as my goal."

In the course of his long career Giggs has a whole catalogue of special goals, most of which he emphatically scored himself, like the quickest United goal ever when he scored against Southampton after 15 seconds in November 1995 on the way to a 4-1 win.

But the goal no United fan will ever forget was the mesmerising winner to beat Arsenal in the FA Cup semi-final replay at Villa Park in April, 1999.

I asked Ryan to talk me through it: "I shall never forget it myself either because it was such a big match and the one people still talk about. I started on the bench but came on after an hour. The game went into extra time and I scored in the 109th minute. I didn't appreciate until I watched it on television exactly what I had done. I thought I was about 30 yards out and I couldn't believe I had run so far with the ball and beaten so many players. It all went so quickly when I was out there and didn't seem so extraordinary. I have got to be honest though and say that when I watched it later I was quite impressed!"

And so he should be! Who can forget the way he pounced on an error by Patrick Vieira to start heading for the Arsenal goal. He left Vieira and Lee Dixon behind before cutting past Martin Keown and beating Dixon again as the full-back tried to cut him off. He then finished with an unstoppable drive to beat David Seaman, whip off his shirt and celebrate by whirring it round over his head. Sir Alex Ferguson remarked: "Our players and fans will be talking about it for years." The manager was spot on there!

Scoring against City to save the blushes of Colin Hendry was his last appearance in the first team that first season, but come the next he established himself as a first-team regular with 32 League starts and six appearances as a substitute. He made his bow in Europe with an appearance in the Cup Winners' Cup and played in every round of the Rumbelows (League) Cup, including the final against Nottingham Forest at Wembley when he set up the winner for Brian McClair that won the game 1-0.

He was still 17 and pretty naïve, as he revealed when he nutmegged Forest's Roy Keane. It wasn't long before Keane had his revenge to send the youngster flying as Giggs recalls: "It was the first time I had come across Keaney. As I lay on the ground he looked down on me and said something to the effect: 'Get up, you soft git.' I tell him now that I sat on the floor thinking who is this muppet!"

Giggs was the first of the youngsters from the revitalised youth set-up to break into the first team. Soon he would be followed by Gary Neville, David Beckham, Nicky Butt, Paul Scholes and Ben Thornley, who in the meantime were on their way to winning the 1992 FA Youth Cup.

Ryan was the captain of the youth team but his first-team duties prevented him playing in many games. He was, though, recalled for the two legs of the final against Crystal Palace, as youth-team manager Eric Harrison fondly remembers: "Winning the Youth Cup was one of the greatest moments of my time in football. It gave me terrific pride and satisfaction to watch that marvellous group of youngsters become the first side to win the trophy for United in 28 years. And they did it in the kind of style befitting a team wearing the famous red shirts.

"Nobody epitomised that side more than Ryan Giggs, who was not only the captain but also one of the guiding lights in a team that had few flaws. He was absolutely brilliant in every youth match he played and it was fitting that it should be he who picked up the trophy at the end of the two-legged final against Crystal Palace.

"He wasn't on his own in that team, but he was the first to step forward into senior football. He has since become one of the world's great players. He could find a place in any team in the world. A great player and a lovely lad, he hasn't changed as a person since he walked through the doors at Old Trafford. He was a natural from the word go and in little or no time everyone at The Cliff training ground was raving about him developing into a world-class player.

"Ryan had the lot and he was so abundantly talented that it would have been a major mystery if he hadn't made it to the top. It's true to say that there have been players who looked certainties to become great stars but somehow failed to reach their potential and fell by the wayside. Nobody expected that to happen to Ryan, who not only possessed all the required ingredients, but also was totally dedicated and single minded in his approach to everything he did.

"I was fortunate to be coach to the young players when Ryan and his contemporaries were making their first steps in the game and I have to say it was a total joy to watch them developing into excellent professional players and fine young men."

Everything happened at a dizzying speed for the emerging Ryan Giggs and he was still only 17 when he made his international debut for Wales in October, 1991. At 17 years and 321 days, he became the youngest-ever Welsh international and he remembers the occasion clearly.

"I came on as a substitute against Germany in Nuremberg. We were losing 4-0 and the score stayed that way – even with me on the field! I think playing for your country is the biggest honour a player can experience and I always relished playing for Wales. It just grieves me that world-class players from Wales like Ian Rush and Mark Hughes have not been able to play in the finals of a major competition."

Giggs saw a stack of players come and go for Wales without ever playing in a team capable of reaching the finals of the European Championship or World Cup. He missed a number of games through injury, and at one point was being criticised in Wales for pulling out of games. Nevertheless, he still won 64 caps before announcing his retirement from international football with the European Championship qualifier against the Czech Republic in Cardiff on June 2, 2007, his final appearance.

It was hardly the record of someone who didn't care for his country, though that last match did rather reflect the path his international career has taken. Giggs played well, indeed the whole team played well, but they were forced to settle for a goalless draw that looks likely to repeat a familiar story – they will fail to qualify for the European finals to leave the World Cup quarter-final under Jimmy Murphy in Sweden way back in 1958 as the last time they figured in the finals of a major tournament.

Ryan almost bowed out with a dream goal after dribbling past four Czech players only for Chelsea goalkeeper Petr Cech to parry his shot. He was given an emotional farewell when he was substituted in the final minutes. "It was great, though it was a shame I couldn't have gone with a win but the fans have been great, from day one right to the end. It's been emotional this week saying goodbye to everyone."

Wales' loss will undoubtedly be United's gain because the decision to quit the international stage was not because he had grown tired of playing for Wales, but an acknowledgement that at the age of 33 he was not getting any younger. As the Wales captain explained: "This decision will keep me fresher throughout the season. The final two months of the last season I hardly trained, it was game, recovery, another game. Now I won't be away on international duty and will be able to train and work at being ready for the next club game. I aim to be fresher and stronger. You can't stand still as an individual and as a team you cannot stand still. And if I want to be involved I need to manage things differently. I hope that next season with the extra rest will give me that edge.

"I felt it was the right time for me and for Wales as well. I've enjoyed training and playing with Wales more over these last couple of years than at any time, even if it has not been as successful as I would have hoped."

The promise of the youthful Giggs was quickly acknowledged by his peers and he was crowned the PFA Young Player of the Year in 1992, and he won the award again the following year.

"I found it very encouraging at that stage of my career. I also remember being very nervous about making a speech," he said.

Inevitably he found himself being described as 'the new George Best', something he found slightly embarrassing, but says: "I think I was only about 15 when the first headline appeared calling me the new George Best, but it never bothered me. I just took it as a compliment. I had never seen him play of course, but my mum and grandparents had and they told me plenty about him. I never let it get to me, though, and simply took it that I was heading in the right direction. I met him quite a few times since and he was always really nice with me."

Of course Ryan always had the advantage of Sir Alex Ferguson as his manager, a man who has never had any problem frightening away the media but who was always helped by the fact that Ryan Giggs never went out of his way to court publicity anyway, as Ryan explains:

"When I first arrived on the first-team scene it coincided with a massive explosion in football with the launch of the Premiership, the impact of Sky Television and the introduction of the Champions League. The game expanded enormously and the players came under the spotlight. I came at the right time for marketing, but I was young and I think I was really helped by the manager sheltering me and limiting what I did with the media. I also felt that at 22, people could easily get sick of seeing me and I didn't want that to happen because I was aiming for another 10 years at least. So I stepped back a bit. The incredible fascination of the media with David Beckham also helped me to lead a quieter life, which suited me.

"I have only known one manager in my time at Old Trafford. Sir Alex brought me to Manchester United and has steered me right the way through. He especially helped me in my younger days, involving me in training with the senior squad at just the right time, playing me in the first team at just the right time, and just as important, resting me at the right time. He is still doing it and I have implicit trust in him. Who wouldn't, as one of his players, after leading us to such sustained success?"

But for all his natural tendency for a quiet life, there still came a defining moment that determined that he wouldn't be going down the celebrity path blazed by his team-mate, David Beckham.

"The high-profile relationship I had with Dani Behr, the TV presenter, was the turning point for me," he explained. "Before I knew it, we were being photographed outside my house and cameramen followed us everywhere. It was very uncomfortable.

"At that point I decided the celebrity lifestyle wasn't for me. Around that time I felt my commercial work was also affecting my football. I thought, 'no, football is my bread and butter. It has to, and always will, come first.'"

Once he had broken into the first team, Ryan didn't have to wait long for his first piece of silverware. After finishing runners-up to Leeds in 1992, the following season saw them win the Premiership by 10 points from Aston Villa and bring the Championship back to Old Trafford for the first time in 26 years. His contribution was considerable, missing only one League game and scoring nine goals.

Ryan Giggs was in on the ground floor of United's most successful era with the honours coming thick and fast. The following year brought a League and FA Cup double and so on until his personal honours board listed 16 major trophies and he had become one of only four players to win three sets of League and FA Cup doubles.

The pinnacle, of course was winning the unique treble in 1999, and naturally a heavy involvement in all three competitions. Sir Alex Ferguson juggled his squad to try and keep everybody fresh for fighting on three fronts with Ryan making 25 appearances in the Premiership, six in the FA Cup and nine in Europe. The challenge of Europe looms large in his life and he has a vivid recollection of the dramatic Champions League final against Bayern Munich, at least the closing stages.

"I remember it for the last two or three minutes. The previous 90 are not worth recalling because frankly it was a bit of a boring game. Once Bayern had scored I think they settled for winning 1-0 with the only chance of increasing their score the occasional breakaway.

"At the same time we were under-performing so it was hardly memorable until injury time when Teddy Sheringham and Ole Solskjaer scored to win us the match. One minute we were thinking we were out of it and then suddenly we had won it. I remember the final for our refusal to accept defeat and then the almighty explosion to snatch victory.

"I like the European atmosphere. The matches are presented in a way that spells out the difference between domestic fixtures and Champions League. I think all the players enjoy the build-up and spectacle. It reminds you of the millions watching around the world, the distinctive music, the Fair Play shaking of hands with your opponents. It adds to the excitement for both the players and the people watching in the stadium and on television."

Although Ryan Giggs has his haul of trophies and completed season 2006-07 in fine style, showing his versatility by playing in midfield, there have also been low moments. For instance, in season 2002-03 his form was at a low ebb with a particularly worrying 1-0 defeat at Blackburn when he was withdrawn in favour of Ole Gunnar Solskjaer to the accompaniment of booing. There was a kind of lethargy to his game which upset a few fans and even had the *Manchester Evening News* inviting readers to join in on their website 'big debate' on Ryan Giggs. Columnist David Sadler, the former United player, urged Sir Alex Ferguson to resist selling him but still felt it necessary to ask him to give the player a rest!

The bleak spell prompted speculation that United might listen to overtures from Italy, but true to form the player kept his head down and came back fighting. At the end of the season he simply said: "I wasn't at my best before Christmas but the boss rested me for a couple of games and I came back fresh and strong. In fact, overall I have probably played the best football of my career.

"I've passed so many landmarks this season. I've played more games than ever before – nearly 60 including those as a substitute – thanks to avoiding any problems with my hamstrings. I have had my best goals tally – 15 in all competitions – for nine years, I passed the 100-goal mark, the 500-appearance mark and I've won my eighth Championship medal. To draw level with Alan Hansen and Phil Neal as the only three players to win eight titles in the history of English football makes me very proud.

"There has been speculation about my future but no-one at the club has said anything to me and as I've said often before I have no intention of leaving. I know what I can do, I know what I can bring to the team and I think I have got better each season with experience. Hopefully that will show again next season when I aim to start the way I have finished this one."

There's no doubt that his tendency to strain his hamstrings has been a big problem throughout his senior career, but he has taken advice and worked hard to overcome what must be one of his few weaknesses. As he once explained to me: "My style is based on speed and sudden bursts, so I think my hamstrings can suffer. Maybe there is a weakness there as well, I'm not sure, but at least the problem has been identified. I do special stretching exercises every day, before and after training, and again before and after matches. The aim is to keep on top of it and for the most part I think we are. The manager is also brilliant at resting me when I start to feel it.

"The way players are advised these days and the way they look after themselves, means that the peak comes later in life than it used to and can be sustained longer."

The player set his sights on winning a record ninth Championship but within a year he had a battle on his hands and it looked as if he might not have the chance. His contract was coming to an end and in keeping with the club's policy for players over 30 were prepared to offer him only a one-year extension. Ryan asked for a three-year agreement and there was a stand-off that seemed to drag on for a long tine. Eventually a compromise was reached and Ryan signed a three-year deal, but one with the third year dependent on the number of games he plays in the first two years.

He will start season 2007-08 needing just 43 appearances to equal Sir Bobby Charlton's all-time record of 759 games in all competitions – and I'm not betting against him achieving his target either!

But really it is Europe that is driving him on, and after picking up his record ninth League title, he is desperate for a second Champions League success.

"Every year seems to bring an even bigger challenge. The prizes get bigger and ambition is also something in your blood. The manager makes sure it stays that way too because if he felt that you had lost your hunger for winning then I don't think you would stay at Old Trafford. He certainly has lost none of his own commitment and passion for success and it filters down to the players

"My ambition is simple, and that's to stay fit, because if I do then I'm sure everything else will fall into place. I think I am playing quite well and if I'm fit I'll be fine. As for afterwards, then I think I'll want to do something within football because that's all I've done since leaving school. I am keeping an open mind on management because you can never be sure who will become a successful manager and who won't. I have seen players who seemed likely to become natural managers fail, and I have seen unlikely characters turn out to be very successful. For instance I never saw Mark Hughes as a manager when he was playing with us at United, but Mark was brilliant for us as manager of Wales."

Settled now with his wife Stacey and two children, Libby and Zach, in a handsome Victorian house in Worsley, the area where he has always lived, he bubbles with enthusiasm about his career with Manchester United as if he was just starting out in the game rather than enjoying life as the 33-year-old elder statesman of Old Trafford.

He believes that Sir Alex is at the start of something big again with the squad he has rebuilt and says: "Potentially this team can be the best in my time with United because of the quality and age of the team.

"There are so many players at the start of their careers or just starting to hit the peak of their form and you can see we have genuinely world-class players in the team. We have the likes of Rio Ferdinand, Cristiano Ronaldo, Wayne Rooney and Nemanja Vidic – that's real quality in the squad and we have quality in depth, too.

"Beating Chelsea to the title was a fantastic achievement. I am sure the hunger is there and, although you need things to go right for you injury-wise, this team can be consistently good over the next five or six years. That means winning the Champions League, not just the Premiership, because being the best in Europe is always something you want to achieve.

"You can't really prioritise, but this season the target was to win the Premiership, then after that the next step is the Champions League."

Having watched Chelsea and Arsenal dominate the Premiership for three years, Ryan might have wondered whether United's glory years had gone for good but his belief in his manager has never wavered and he believes big things are around the corner again.

"Over the past three years this team has been developing and it's definitely been good enough, except it lacked the consistency of Chelsea and Arsenal. They deserved to win titles and we didn't, but I think we deserved it this year. We've played great football but also been consistent and had that bit of steel, too.

"You do worry because I'd never gone three years without winning the title, but I was optimistic seeing the ability and hunger in the squad and a good mix between experienced players who'd won it and the hunger of players who hadn't.

"The test now is to go on winning. We've produced great football, but it's no use producing great performances without winning anything. But we have got that taste of success again and I'm sure the players have got the determination to go on and win more.

"As far as I am concerned they have given me a fresh lease of life. There are certain players who give you a buzz from watching them play, like Cristiano and Wayne. I've got a real buzz, too, seeing the faces of the lads who have won their first Championship. I remember when I won my first Championship – it's the best feeling in the world!"

But that's history and Ryan keeps his medals in the Manchester United museum where he feels they belong because it's the future that is important to him.

Ryan Giggs will always have time for people along the way, though, as you can perhaps judge from his testimonial match against Glasgow Celtic in 2001 when he led the teams out with his young sister Bethany by his side and explained to me: "I have always been close to Bethany and I thought it would be nice for her. Players who get testimonials are usually older than me and they can involve their children. I hadn't any children then but I did have a nice sister. I have a brother as well, Rhodri, but he is a bit older and I don't think he would have appreciated me leading him out by the hand!

"The whole night bowled me over. I was stunned by the massive crowd, and though it's usually the money people think about when a testimonial is mentioned, it's the appreciation of the fans that gets to you. I couldn't believe how good it was."

There was further appreciation for Ryan Giggs in the Queen's Birthday Honours of June 2007, when he was awarded the OBE for services to sport. It was nothing less than he deserved because this man not only plays football rather well, he plays life rather well, too!

RYAN GIGGS - CAREER STATS

BORN:	Cardiff
DATE OF BIRTH:	November 29, 1973
JOINED UNITED:	July 1990
UNITED LEAGUE APPS:	504
GOALS:	99
INT. CAPS (Wales):	64
GOALS:	12

1991-2003

David
Beckham

There is no doubt that David Beckham is the most famous footballer on the planet. That's not to say he is the greatest player and indeed in terms of talent and ability he was certainly not an automatic choice for my Perfect 10, particularly when you consider the calibre of people I have left out.

He is a very, very good footballer of course and he's had his great moments – for instance, who can forget his inspired performance and winning free-kick against Greece at Old Trafford that took England to the World Cup in Japan and South Korea – but his celebrity status has always loomed larger than his ranking as a player.

Indeed, his image as an icon has been a distraction and the managers of Manchester United, Real Madrid and England all decided at some point that they couldn't be doing with Beckham the cult celebrity, subsequently booting him out of their teams.

Two of them were left with egg on their faces. Fabio Capello dropped him from his struggling side at the Bernabeu and famously said he would not play for Real Madrid again. Capello called him "half an actor" and had difficulty coming to terms with the high-flying distractions that always seemed to come into the Beckham life, like the invitation to fly to Rome for Tom Cruise's wedding. Capello wasn't happy and told his player to be back in 24 hours, which meant Victoria had to attend the service and the big party afterwards on her own.

It seemed that they might be going to America sooner than planned after announcing that he had signed a five-year contract worth £25m a year for LA Galaxy. The player was forced to train on his own and Capello said: "David will continue to train but won't play any more. He's always been a model professional, but after he signed such an important contract with another team we cannot count on him. You can't pretend to have the same enthusiasm when your head is elsewhere."

However, it's a mistake to write off David Beckham where football is concerned because, while he is a moth pulled to the bright lights of fashion and style, he always takes his football seriously. He had to train on his own but with great strength of character he came through and with Real still struggling Capello changed his mind and restored him to his ailing team.

David had been in the doghouse but he returned as the inspiration behind a Madrid revival that saw his team win five games in a row to close the gap on Barcelona at the top of the table. Capello was now saying after a typical Beckham display: "Yet again the Englishman was the decisive player. He was a titan, he gave us a festival of measured passing. At times it seemed he would win the game on his own."

Then on the final day of the season Real Madrid beat Real Mallorca to pip Barcelona for the La Liga title and enable Beckham to say a golden goodbye to Spain. It was his first major trophy in his four years in Spain and achieved in the nick of time. David described it as an incredible feeling and said: "I couldn't have dreamt it any better than to leave with a trophy."

The conclusion is clear, as his England recall also confirmed, that you should never dismiss Beckham lightly. There is substance behind the froth of the celebrity circus, and as the fuss and furore once more flared up, the player simply said: "I have enjoyed my time in Spain. I don't regret my move to Real Madrid. I wanted to go to a club like this, to one of the biggest clubs in the world and I've lived a kid's dream really to be able to play with the likes of Zidane, Ronaldo, Roberto Carlos, Raul and Figo."

So why go to the States, hardly the cutting edge of football, at the relatively young age of 32? He says: "I wanted a different challenge, and for me the biggest challenge was going to America and playing in the MLS (Major League Soccer) and living a different lifestyle. I'm looking forward to that."

In actual fact, a move to the glitz and glamour of Los Angeles, the home of Hollywood, is a logical move for Becks and Posh after moving steadily nearer a celebrity lifestyle through his career, and in America he will enjoy the best of both worlds. He will still be a competitive sportsman, albeit at a level that will enable him to carry on playing for a good few years yet, but without the relentless pressure, mental as well as physical, that goes with clubs like Manchester United and Real Madrid.

At the same time he and his wife and their three children Brooklyn, Romeo and Cruz, can enjoy the trappings of fame and fortune in a part of the world that is the epitome of the high life and which is welcoming the Beckhams with open arms.

Already David has been pictured as a knight riding a white charger, cloak flying, sword in one hand and shield in the other, in a high-profile endorsement for *Disney*. There's talk of films with lessons lined up to lower the pitch of his voice while he studies method acting. David and Victoria will be in their element, however much some of the English football pundits huff and puff that he is leaving serious football too soon.

Steve McClaren crossed swords with Beckham soon after his appointment as England manager. He accepted the player's resignation as captain following the disappointing World Cup campaign in Germany in 2006 and followed up by leaving him out of his first England squad, a new broom sweeping clean and clearly keen to make his point that England had a new boss and were entering a new era.

But with England still struggling he did a U-turn and brought him back for a friendly against Brazil in May 2007 and on the basis of an outstanding display kept him in the side for the European Championship qualifier against Estonia the following month. Beckham rose to the occasion, just as he had done in Madrid, and with pin-point crosses from the right wing, always one of his specialities, he created two of the goals in the 3-0 win that put England back on track to qualify for the European Championships in 2008.

Once again Beckham fever – and what else can you call it – swept the country to the point that actor and comedian Russell Brand sarcastically wrote in his *Guardian* column: "It's been interesting to view the latest instalment of the Beckham saga, his reinstatement first to the team and then to his position of national darling and soccer-Christ."

David's dramatic comeback reignited the hullabaloo that followed his initial decision to walk away from European football to go to America and play for LA Galaxy.

Apparently finished at Real Madrid, a move to America seemed quite logical for a man sucked more and more into the razzmatazz of Hollywood. Victoria, as the 'Posh' part of the *Spice Girls* singing group, has never left showbiz and with a sophisticated publicity machine behind her never missing a trick, the States seemed the next logical step.

It seemed that the media were just about reconciled to see Beckham on his way to a more glitzy life but the success of his return for England now poses the question of whether his domestic football will be good enough to keep him at international standard. The player has certainly re-established himself and it would be impossible for Steve McClaren to drop him before he at least has had the chance to make four more international appearances and become a 100-cap player. His team-mates have certainly rallied round with Frank Lampard typically enthusing: "He still has something to offer England next season, no matter what league he is in. When he is playing like he is it doesn't matter where he is making his living. He could be playing in the park with his mates but I'd still have him in my team because when he delivers balls with that right foot he makes goals."

Peter Crouch says it is fantastic for him to have David back and Michael Owen added after scoring against Estonia: "His quality is undoubted. He is the best crosser in the world. He has great vision and he is a great passer. It was a cracking ball for my goal."

Sir Alex Ferguson was the first of course to experience the roller coaster ride with Beckham and was the first to decide that pursuing a show business lifestyle with his wife Victoria clashed with what he wanted from one of his players. It was not just the damage he was doing to himself as the way it affected his team-mates. I believe the United manager could see problems ahead, and always decisive when he sees danger, he decided to sell him to Real Madrid. I think he felt Beckham was becoming a distraction in the dressing room and that before long his team-mates would look on him with resentment.

He certainly didn't want the kind of situation that built up in Germany at the World Cup when the 'Wags' commanded as much attention as the players. Ferguson is a great family man but I don't think he sees himself as someone needing to manage the wives and girlfriends as well as the team.

He had long been irritated by the way David was becoming more and more a celebrity figure and I recall the exasperation in his voice when he described the tracksuit his player had worn for training one day. "It was all sparkly, he looked like Gary Glitter," he declared.

In his mind, Ferguson had already met the player halfway and had accepted David's avant-garde style, his constantly changing hairstyles ranging from a Mohican to cornrows, or as one newspaper headline put it: '*Who's the prat in the plait?*'

His way-out dressing saw him at one point wearing a sarong and he also took to wearing an Alice band to keep his long hair out of his eyes. I believe Fergie asked him at one point to stop wearing Alice bands because it was too 'girlie', but he backed off, accepting that times had moved on from his days growing up in Glasgow!

He put his foot down though, when David failed to arrive for training one day in the season after winning the treble just before a key game against Leeds United. The player offered as his excuse that his little son, Brooklyn, was ill and that he had had to stay at home to look after him. The manager took the view that David and Victoria could have made alternative arrangements and it did look rather like the tail attempting to wag the dog, even if the feminists might ask why it is always the wife who has to take responsibility for the childcare. Fergie might be a confirmed socialist and he is definitely a family man but he still has some quite conservative views and David's excuse didn't wash.

Although it was a risk because the game involved was at Leeds who were a power in those days, Fergie nevertheless sent David home when he came in the following day and because he hadn't taken part in the preparations for the match he didn't pick him to play. United in fact won 1-0 without him, but more importantly the manager had made a point and at the time Ferguson thought he had got David back on the straight and narrow, and more focused on football.

Much was read into the flying boot incident when after a poor performance an angry manager took a kick at a boot that hit David on the forehead. David didn't seem to make much of an effort to disguise the sticking plaster and some people tried to make out that Fergie had done it deliberately. My view was that it was akin to throwing teacups across the dressing room and that the player just happened to be in the way.

David refused to comment and the manager, at his stubborn

best, was certainly not going to apologise. People drew their own conclusions but it was certainly another nail in the player's time at Old Trafford.

His departure from Old Trafford was muted, sadly so considering the role he had played in helping to bring Manchester United and Sir Alex Ferguson the most successful era in the history of the club. Who could have guessed the ending when you look back to the early days and the way David left home in London for a life in Manchester.

It was thanks to a tip-off from Sir Bobby Charlton, the Manchester United and England legend, that David Beckham came to Old Trafford. The former United captain and international star, who is now a director at Old Trafford, used to run coaching schools for youngsters and over the years has steered a number of youngsters to his former club.

But Beckham, though always a United fan as a schoolboy, had a secret fear living in London two hundred miles away from Manchester and used to say to his mother: "Manchester United will never find me down here so far away from Manchester."

One day, though, after playing for his local junior team Ridgeway Rovers, he was greeted by the news he had been longing for. Mum Sandra was at the game and remembers:

"I stood waiting outside the changing rooms. He was always the last out and when he finally emerged I just said to him: 'It was a good job you had a good game.' 'Why was that,' he asked. I replied that the Manchester United scout had been at the match and that he was coming round to the house later. He jumped up in the air and cried because he had always been worried that United wouldn't find him in London."

Of course, the more local clubs had also been aware of Beckham's potential and he had been invited for trials at Leyton Orient, the London Third Division club. Then slightly against his inclinations he signed forms for the school of excellence at Spurs. It was a move which delighted his granddad, a Tottenham supporter, but David and his dad Ted knew it was a move designed only so that he could get better coaching and make progress.

His heart still lay with Manchester United and after a number of invitations north during the Easter and Summer school holidays he signed schoolboy forms for Manchester United on his 14th birthday. Manager Sir Alex Ferguson was aware that it would be a big step to bring a young boy from 200 miles away to live in digs in Manchester, so he always made a point of keeping in touch with him. Every time United played in the London area, the Beckham family would be invited to the game.

As former captain Steve Bruce recalls: "This weedy, spiky-haired kid always seemed to be hanging about. Every time we went to London he was there sniffing about. One day in the dressing room at the League Cup final at Wembley he was picking up the boots and putting them into the skip just to be involved. We knew at the time from the treatment he was getting that he must be a bit special."

Rival clubs, especially Tottenham, didn't like it when David walked out on them to play for Manchester United, but the player never had any doubts. George Best, when he was young, ran away back to Belfast because he was homesick and Sir Matt Busby had to persuade him to return, but Beckham always felt Manchester was his second home.

"The first time I came to Manchester I just knew it was the place for me. I just felt right. The fact that the manager treated me like one of his own sons made it easier. My dad and mum have always been United fans and I think they were chuffed when I came to Old Trafford, but they didn't push me. They always said it was up to me."

At the height of those happy early days David told me: "What I know is that I love it up in Manchester. I don't expect I'll ever lose my London Cockney accent, and I don't want to, but joining Manchester United was the best move I could have made."

When it came time to leave school at 16, United offered him a six-year deal, two years on the club's youth training scheme, two years as an apprentice and then a minimum two years as a professional.

His father, Ted, said: "When David heard the offer he jumped 10 feet in the air and started screaming: 'That's what I've always wanted.'"

Although England's schoolboy selectors had decided he was too small and slender to play at international level, he soon won a place in the young United side which won the FA Youth Cup in 1992 packed with the starlets like Ryan Giggs, Gary Neville, Paul Scholes and Nicky Butt who went on to win the unique treble and play for England, or in the case of Ryan Giggs, for Wales.

The manager still thought the slim-line Beckham needed toughening up and so he was farmed out on loan to Preston North End, a move that worried the player.

"When players went on loan I thought it was because their clubs didn't rate them. The manager said it would do me good though and in fact I loved it there. The players were brilliant with me and though they obviously reckoned I was cocky and over-confident at first they soon treated me like one of them."

Beckham came back stronger and made his first-team debut as a substitute at Brighton in the League Cup at the start of season 1992-93, but he had to wait two more years before getting another chance. Season 1994-95 saw him make seven first-team appearances plus three as a substitute, though he did score his first goal, netting in a 4-0 win at home against Galatasaray in the Champions League.

The following season saw him getting into full stride. He came on as a half-time substitute for Phil Neville in the opening game and scored in the 3-1 defeat to Aston Villa at Villa Park.

Alan Hansen famously said on television that "you don't win anything with kids" following this result but Beckham stayed in the side along with the other youngsters, United won their next five matches and then came with a rush at the end of the season to pip Kevin Keegan's Newcastle for the Championship. David made 26 League appearances plus seven as a substitute and scored seven times.

He also scored the winner against Chelsea at Villa Park to put his team through to the final of the FA Cup at Wembley, where Eric Cantona scored to beat Liverpool and give David Beckham a League and FA Cup double in what was really his first season as a regular.

Goals were becoming his speciality as he demonstrated on the opening day of the next season, 1996-97, at Selhurst Park when he spotted Wimbledon goalkeeper Neil Sullivan had come off his line. He let fly from just inside his own half to score a 60-yard goal that became one of the defining moments of his career. Photographers and David Beckham go together like salt and pepper and naturally the BBC *Match of the Day* cameras were there to record the first of many super goals.

Says David: "I honestly meant to do it. I saw the goalkeeper off his line and so I just had a go. To be fair I struck it well and a curve towards the end got the keeper. He told me at the end of the game that he thought it was a great goal. The ball seemed to be in the air for ages and then the place just erupted. It changed my football life."

Free-kicks, hit with pace and remarkable swerve, became his trademark and in those days Alex Ferguson felt free to pay handsome tribute to his prodigy: "David is Britain's finest striker of a football, not because of God-given talent, but because he practises with a relentless application the majority of less gifted players would not contemplate."

David picked up his second Championship medal and also marked that season by winning his first England cap, playing against Moldova in September, 1996 and holding his place all the way to the World Cup in France the following summer.

The tournament turned out to be a disaster for Glenn Hoddle's

England and for David in particular. He became the villain of the piece following his dismissal against Argentina and he came home as a scapegoat for England's failure. He was subjected to unbelievable abuse but David came through the biggest test of his career an even stronger person to play some of his best football, a truly incredible achievement.

He mastered the temperament that had let him down when he made the retaliatory and petulant flick at Diego Simeone to find himself dismissed and England down to 10 men. Even Glenn Hoddle seemed ready to seize on Beckham's departure as a convenient excuse for England's downfall. Most fair-minded people accepted that England failed for far more serious reasons but I'm sure that is not how it must have felt at the time standing in Beckham's boots! He was vilified mercilessly, especially at West Ham on the first away League trip of the new season, where they were burning his effigy.

He says now: "Some people seemed to think it a real crime but I never saw it that way. I have got to be honest and say that I never even felt guilty because everyone makes mistakes in football and what I did was hardly outrageous. Let's face it, I had never been sent off before. I'm not a violent person, but the United supporters certainly helped me.

"I noticed the clapping in the first game I played back at Old Trafford when I walked to the corner flag near the visiting fans who were all jeering. I couldn't help but be aware of it because of all the stick I had been taking, and it was very moving. It was kind of like a standing ovation and I couldn't help smiling.

"It meant a lot to me after everything that had happened and the way the United supporters stuck with me was unbelievable. During and after the World Cup there was a lot of criticism and all kinds of things were going on, but as soon as I got back to Old Trafford I realised there were still people who liked and loved me.

"It had crossed my mind that going abroad might be one way

of getting some peace but I soon realised that I didn't want to be anywhere but Old Trafford. Alex Ferguson was very supportive. He phoned me the day after it happened and he also rang my mum and dad, which was brilliant because they were not used to 20 or 30 film crews outside their house waiting for me to arrive home from France."

So with the help of manager and fans Beckham held his nerve as United steadily mounted their bid to win the treble of League, FA Cup and Champions League. There was a new maturity being displayed by Beckham and the other young players responding to the experience gained from playing with Eric Cantona, and Beckham continued to play an important part in the three-pronged attack for honours. He played mostly as the wide-right player with something of a licence to roam and always honing his ability to whip in crosses from the right wing, which proved a nightmare for opposing defences.

His crossing excellence was never more in evidence than in the first leg of the key European quarter-final against Inter Milan. Twice he dipped in searing centres for Dwight Yorke to score with headers in a 2-0 win before helping the team to play comfortably for a 1-1 draw in the San Siro Stadium to go through to the semi-finals against Juventus.

Beckham's crossing was again instrumental in undermining the Italians as United drew 1-1 in the first leg against Juve at Old Trafford before reaching the final with a superb 3-2 fighting victory in Turin. In between those two European ties, he put in a super-strike against Arsenal to set United up for a 2-1 semi-final replay victory that took the Reds into the final of the FA Cup.

Then began an electric 11 days of trophy hunting with David Beckham taking his game to an even higher plane with decisive moments which saw Alex Ferguson's team clinch the unique treble.

First up for grabs was the League title with a showdown

against Spurs at Old Trafford. David Ginola, the Tottenham winger who had been voted Player of the Year by both the Players' Association and the Football Writers, was lined up against them, but Beckham made it clear who was the real player of the year. Les Ferdinand put the visitors ahead with an early goal but Beckham put United back into the game with a powerful shot just before half-time, and with the help of a goal from sub Andy Cole the Championship came to Old Trafford.

The following weekend it was the FA Cup at stake with Newcastle the opposition and United seemingly in early trouble when Gary Speed put Roy Keane out of the game with a damaged ankle. Teddy Sheringham took his place but the key move was switching Beckham into Keane's role in central midfield.

Beckham teamed up with Paul Scholes in the middle of the park to run the game and underline his growing confidence as well as his transformation from villain at the start of the season to hero. He never stopped running, passing and prompting as he revelled in his midfield role, and even after Speed had caught him in the face with his boot, he kept his temper and composure.

It was his 58th game of the season and he had manager Alex Ferguson purring after the 2-0 victory had clinched a double: "I have rested most of the players at some stage of the season, but not David Beckham. I have played him throughout it all, but then, I know his nature. I know he has the best stamina of any player at the club. He has had fantastic energy since being a young boy and despite everything he has been through, I have never doubted him.

"After Roy Keane's injury, David moved into the central role alongside Paul Scholes and the pair of them responded magnificently. I thought Beckham was brilliant, tremendous, in the FA Cup final. He's a great player but he also has an incredible appetite for the game, and when you have ability harnessed to work rate you can hardly ask for anything more.

"He enjoys the game so much and always has. I think he became a better player last season, but then again, we expected that of our younger players. David is now 24 and approaching the mature years of his career. Some players unfortunately don't fulfil their promise but David most certainly has. He has been faced with a lot of potential distractions but the main thing he wants to do is play football. He gets a lot of attention but he has handled it."

Beckham's display at Wembley softened the blow of being without the suspended Roy Keane and Paul Scholes for the European final against Bayern Munich in Barcelona.

Ferguson summed up the mood when he said: "People are saying that to go to the Nou Camp without Roy Keane will be an uphill task. Yes, we will be without Paul Scholes as well, but David Beckham is just dying to show what he can do."

The suspensions prompted Ferguson to keep Beckham in the middle and after going behind to an early goal from Bayern, it looked as if it might have been the wrong selection. There was nothing lacking in Beckham's individual performance though, and it all came right in the end, thanks to that glorious last-ditch revival in injury time that typically had Beckham showing the way.

Playing with a frenzied urgency, yet ice-cool when it came to the delivery of two superbly-hit corner-kicks, Beckham's first cross was headed in by Teddy Sheringham for an equaliser and then he delivered a second corner for Ole Solskjaer's winner.

Beckham had lifted United to European glory and a fabulous treble and told me: "I will never forget the last few minutes. Time was up and of course Bayern Munich were in front. I looked round and saw that the trophy was on its way down ready for presentation with the Bayern colours draped on it.

"A couple of minutes later I had my hands on it and it was ours. When I was a boy I used to watch on television and see people picking up the European Cup. I used to think it was big, but not as big as it actually is, or as brilliant.

"It's always special to play for your club in Europe. I was thrilled when I first saw Old Trafford dressed up for a big night in the Champions League because there is definitely a different atmosphere for a European match.

"Everything in the build-up helps make it all the more special. Walking to the centre circle with the opposition team, the music, the shaking hands with your opponents, all give you a tingle and I think the fans love it as well.

"I shall never forget my debut in Europe because I had the good fortune to mark it with a goal against Galatasaray at Old Trafford in December, 1994. The ball was rolled back to me, and although I didn't hit it as cleanly as I might, it went in to crown a great night in a match we won 4-0. It was a good start in Europe for me.

"The game I remember most though has got to be the night we came back from two goals down in Turin to beat Juventus 3-2 in the semi-final second leg. I guess everyone wrote us off when we went two-down so early in the game. It's certainly not what you want, but we got a first goal, then a second and took command to score a winner. I shall never forget it.

"The final itself was of course also unforgettable. It was difficult at first to take in, but the crowd soon convinced me that we had done it. It was the most exciting atmosphere I have ever experienced and the first thing I did at the end was to run to our supporters. I like to celebrate with the fans because I think they deserve a piece of the action."

While the treble season was the undoubted high point of David's United career, he continued to help them win silverware. They retained the Championship for two more seasons, missed a year but won it back from Arsenal in season 2002-03 to bring down the curtain on David's United career and trigger his transfer to Real Madrid.

The fans were divided, some still so much in love with his football that they wanted him to stay at any price; others could understand the manager coming to the conclusion that managing David Beckham was a job in itself and that the celebrity sideshow was in danger of becoming the main event. Despite protestations from the player and his family, I think Fergie also felt that behind the scenes moves were already afoot to get him to Spain and if there's one thing that Ferguson insists upon, it's total commitment from his players.

His final game for United was against Everton at Goodison Park on May 11, 2003. He left with a flourish by scoring from a free-kick in a 2-1 win. All told he had played 265 League games for United and scored 62 goals, sharing in the club's most successful-ever era.

Although his departure seemed to drag on for ages, he had not been able to say farewell to the fans, but this was put right when he returned to Old Trafford for UEFA's exhibition match against a European team staged to mark United's half-century of participation in European competition.

Injury prevented him from captaining the European side but he went out on to the pitch at half-time to tell the 73,000 crowd: "I have waited four years for this. The one thing I have looked forward to since I left is going back to say goodbye to the fans because I never really had the chance to do that. I always feel that Old Trafford is my home, my rightful home. I'm obviously from London but I spent so many years there and it's my club. It's the club I have always supported and the club I will always support. It's the best stadium in the world for me. The Bernabeu is incredible, but United is the club where I feel I grew up."

Then he went on to pay tribute to Sir Alex Ferguson: "You have the best manager in the world at this club. And you have a team that can win things not just this season but for many years to come. I wouldn't be the player and the person I am today without the manager. It's been well documented that we had our ups and downs, but I owe almost everything to him. Obviously I had strong parents and a strong family behind me, but without him giving me the opportunity to get into the United team I wouldn't be the player I am today and wouldn't have achieved and won a lot of the things I have."

Sir Alex was equally gracious on the night when he said: "I expected him to get a great reception. He had great years here. He was a great player." As kiss-and-make-up tales go, there was hardly a dry eye in the house!

So now David and his family are embarking on a new life in America, and, it has got to be said, earning an even bigger fortune, but I think football will still play a big part in his life and perhaps we shouldn't rubbish the game in the States.

As Alexi Lalas, former Serie A footballer and now President of LA Galaxy says: "I get so irritated when I hear the experts in England talk about David Beckham as if he's going into semi-retirement by leaving Real Madrid for Los Angeles. That's ignorance of the first degree because almost every single one of those critics has not even seen a single MLS game. It's insulting to us and to our sport to say Beckham is on his way to Hollywood when he's coming to play in one of the most competitive leagues in the world."

We will see, but one thing for sure, Manchester United fans will wish him well!

DAVID BECKHAM - CAREER STATS	
BORN:	Leytonstone
DATE OF BIRTH:	May 2 1975
JOINED UNITED:	July 1991
UNITED LEAGUE APPS:	265
GOALS:	62
INT. CAPS (England):	96
GOALS:	17

2003-

Cristiano Ronaldo

Compared with the rest of my Perfect 10, Cristiano Ronaldo is very much the new boy on the block, and in football terms, still wet behind the ears; normally I would look for a bit more service before considering a player for a place in such a distinguished team. But how can I ignore a player who has hit British football with such a refreshing zing and taken the art of beating an opponent to a new level?

His impact at Old Trafford, and indeed on the game generally, has been stunning and there is a substance to his style that I believe will see him continue to prosper to the point that there will be no doubting his right to be considered as one of Manchester United's all-time great players.

He swept the honours board in 2006-07, culminating in him being voted the Professional Footballers' Association Player of the Year and then running away with the Football Writers' Association award as the outstanding man of the season.

At United's own end-of-season awards dinner the Portuguese youngster was also voted the Players' Player of the Year and was then up on the rostrum a second time to receive a similar accolade from the fans. In fact he must have lost count of the number of awards that came his way from admiring supporters, so it was all the more refreshing to hear him telling his team-mates at the club's function: "I try to learn and improve." The honours were not served up to him on a plate. It took character and determination to recover from a fractious and controversial summer playing for Portugal in the World Cup in Germany.

His problem came in the quarter-final against England on July 8. You remember the scenario when Wayne Rooney tangled with Ricardo Carvalho and trod on him? Whether deliberately or accidentally only Rooney really knows, but the referee deemed it violent play and out came the red card. Cristiano turned to the Portugal bench and with a half smile on his face comes up with the infamous wink. Some thought that Ronaldo had also tried to get Rooney sent off.

The cameras all caught the wink and it didn't go down well. It was considered sneaky and underhand, certainly not very British! *The Sun* newspaper pictured a cut-out dartboard with the wink featuring as the bull's-eye and the invitation to throw darts. It was all rather similar to the way David Beckham had been pilloried after the World Cup in France eight years earlier.

And just as Beckham had been made the scapegoat for England's penalty shootout defeat against Argentina, so Ronaldo was blamed for England losing against Portugal in a similar fashion. And it wasn't just English supporters making him out the villain of the piece. Four days after the England game he was booed every time he touched the ball playing against France in the semi-final. The Portuguese lost but Ronaldo was easily the best player on the pitch, somehow able to put the furore out of his mind.

The problem was that the wink was only the beginning as speculation and rumour went round like wildfire that he was fed-up with playing in England and that he wanted to go to Spain. One paper alleged that Rooney was ready to throttle his team-mate on their return to Old Trafford, and another player said that if he were Rooney he would punch him the next time they met.

Ronaldo was quoted as saying that he felt he should get out

of Manchester and that his destination would be Real Madrid or Barcelona. It was an unsettling period for him after the disappointment of his country's semi-final defeat, but Ronaldo has character and strength of mind to match his talent.

He says he had to take a step back and see things through, but that now he can look back with satisfaction that he coped OK. "After the game and Wayne Rooney's deserved sending off, we met. He came to me and told me: 'Cristiano, well played. You had a good game, you have a great team, I wish you luck for the rest of the competition!' In the following days, we exchanged texts. Even during holidays. Like buddies. At the same time, they said that Rooney was angry with me. My relationship with Wayne is the opposite of that, it's top. We are like brothers. We're the same age. He also has great talent. We get on really well.

"Everyone does what he has to do for his country and I did what I had to do. We were on opposite sides at the World Cup. But now there's no problem. There are no personal differences. It's all in the past. It's not an issue, it's gone and life goes on."

What about all the reports that he was ready to leave Old Trafford? Does he have any doubts about his future with Manchester United?

He said: "It didn't take me long to realise that I'd done nothing wrong. I defended my country, my colours. This is what is most important to me. Reactions were fierce after that match and Rooney's sending off, but they didn't get to me. At Manchester, from Ferguson to the players, everybody welcomed and supported me at the highest point of the controversy."

Did he see the London tabloid with his face being made a target for a darts game?

"Everybody talked about it so I ended up seeing it, but I don't care," he replied.

Of course, the winking issue was not the only problem Cristiano has had to deal with since joining Manchester United for £12.24m from Sporting Lisbon in August 2003. Right from the start he had a habit of going to ground a little too easily for many people's liking, and he soon won a reputation as 'a diver'.

Naturally Sir Alex Ferguson defended him vigorously but I think privately he talked to the player and reminded him that he was courting trouble and would certainly make himself very unpopular if he didn't make more effort to stay on his feet. Apart from referees clamping down on diving, he explained, it was not something that he wanted to see at Manchester United.

Cristiano did in fact take the advice on board and he cut out his tendency to look for a free-kick or penalty every time he was touched, however slightly. Inevitably though because of his speed and the delicate nature of his trickery, he continued to be fouled a lot.

He won a penalty on his debut for United after coming on as a 60th-minute substitute against Bolton at Old Trafford. He had only been on the pitch a few minutes, but like many more opponents would discover, he was difficult to contain and it was only too easy for defenders to miss the ball and make contact.

The issue of diving eased but did not disappear, especially as far as Middlesbrough were concerned with their manager Gareth Southgate especially angered by the player's style. In a way you can understand because in season 2006-07 United played Middlesbrough four times in the Premiership and FA Cup and three of the games were decided by penalties involving Ronaldo in United's favour.

As they prepared for the fourth meeting Ferguson felt he had to redress the balance of Southgate's criticism and he delivered a barely-coded message in his programme notes for the game at Old Trafford, no doubt hoping that the referee would read them as well as the visiting manager who he suggested had become paranoid about Ronaldo.

He wrote: 'Brace yourselves...we are in for a tough time this evening! Middlesbrough are an aggressive side and I believe it will be quite physical out there.

'We have had some contentious games with our visitors already this season and the arguments all seem to spring from how Gareth Southgate and his players perceive Cristiano Ronaldo.

'Everyone has a view and I concede it must be highly frustrating to play against him and equally maddening to find penalties costing you dearly.

'All three league and cup games between Middlesbrough and us so far this season have been decided by penalties and we have had some great hullabaloos. It is easy in that kind of situation to become paranoid.

'For me, though, the diving issue has been blown out of all proportion. It is only too easy to allege diving as an excuse for failing to cope with Cristiano's speed and flying feet.

'The biggest row came after our last match in the FA Cup sixth-round replay at Old Trafford when Ronaldo was tripped and scored the resulting penalty for our 1-0 win. It was a clear penalty but Middlesbrough didn't see it that way and clearly found it difficult to accept the decision. *Sky* didn't help by fanning the flames but you can't do much about that because controversy makes good viewing.

'What did sadden me after James Morrison had been sent off for kicking Ronaldo's legs from under him was the comment from the Middlesbrough camp that that was what the rest of the team had wanted to do throughout the match.

'Hopefully wiser counsel will now have prevailed, though I did wonder what would have happened if someone from United had made that kind of remark. Would the FA have let it go if it had come from one of my players or from me?

'I somehow doubt it, but that's the FA and now I hope we can have a game without incident; my other wish is that we have some strong refereeing. Players like Ronaldo deserve protection, and as I say, given their grievances, I don't expect

Middlesbrough will be holding back today. We are in for a hard one!'

As it turned out, the game was drawn 1-1 and passed without incident as far as Ronaldo was concerned. Kieran Richardson scored for United while Mark Viduka got the Middlesbrough equaliser that slowed United's Championship challenge – but didn't stop it.

Ferguson later explained to me: "When you are attempting Cristiano's kind of high jinks on the ball at such great speed it doesn't take much of a nudge to knock you off balance and send you flying, and that's not diving.

"We don't encourage players to cheat at this club and Cristiano knows that; at the same time we don't encourage players to kick lumps out of their opponents, and Ronaldo is the most fouled player in the game. It says a lot for him that he doesn't complain, he just picks himself up and gets on with it."

My view is that Ronaldo is perfectly entitled to make the most of situations when full-backs are closing in. Defenders are not always very sporting with their 'stop-him-at-all-costs' tactics and sometimes he has to jump and dodge to avoid serious injury; and if in the process of trying to avoid a heavy tackle he loses his balance and falls over, then he has every right to look for a free-kick or penalty. It's tough and it's a battle out there, and Cristiano Ronaldo needs to use everything he can think of to get the better of those hard guys trying to nail him!

I do sometimes worry for Ronaldo's safety, especially after watching the red mist descend on James Morrison in the Middlesbrough game, but Sir Alex doesn't seem unduly concerned on that score and tells me: "Fortunately referees these days do their best to protect talented players, although Ronaldo was fouled nine times in the FA Cup tie at Middlesbrough. It shouldn't have been allowed to continue like that, but certainly things have improved compared with the days when you see clips of George Best and the cynical attempts to hack him down.

"Standards have improved and though Morrison's attempted retribution does make you wonder, I think players generally have too much respect and admiration for a player like Ronaldo to set out seriously to injure him. They'll try to stop him one way or another but not break his leg or anything like that. That's not a worry for me."

I hope the United manager is right, not only for the pain it would cause Ronaldo, but because it would damage the most thrilling and entertaining player now on view in English football.

Ronaldo himself does not seem unduly concerned about the diving sneers and simply says: "I'm convinced that it's that reputation that lost me the best young player title of the 2006 World Cup. But all these accusations don't bother me at all. Journalists would do better to talk about the brutalities that I suffer during games. And those who whistle at me when they think I'm diving, somehow I can thank them for they give me even more motivation. When I feel the hostility, I say to myself that if people whistle it's because they're afraid of me, and so, that I'm good and dangerous."

Hand-in-hand with Cristiano's tendency to tumble goes of course his ability for trickery on the ball. In particular his step-over technique as he waves his foot over the ball, not once but perhaps several times, sometimes on the run, often standing still and as if it's a magic wand he's wafting rather than a foot, opponents are apt to go into some kind of trance, and then he's away.

George Best was pretty good at mesmerising defenders but generally speaking this kind of high-quality technique is not typical of British football and in his early days he was treated with some suspicion. It was said in some quarters that he was a show pony with one trick that would soon be hammered out of him. But this boy has both strength and conviction, and he survived the cynicism, the criticism and the plans that were devised to stop him.

Ronaldo has always liked to dribble as he recently explained to Erik Bielderman of the French sports newspaper *L'Equipe*, who wanted to know what goes through his mind when he is on one of his amazing runs.

"I think about nothing. Dribbling is natural to me. I was born a dribbler. It's my style, it's my life. My mind is inhabited by simple thoughts: to give the best of myself and remain focused," he replied.

L'Equipe pressed the point: "Yes, but still, when you eliminate two or three defenders, don't you have the vision of a toreador succeeding with his passes?"

Said Cristiano: "I like the idea but I don't think like this at all. Dribbles must be constructive for the team. I don't want to dribble just for the sake of it. I know I can be selfish. I do like having the ball. I know, too, that sometimes I show off. And I lose the ball. But it's coming, it's coming. Year-on-year, I'm becoming more realistic, stronger. I know better now when to choose to pass the ball. Still, I'm not afraid to keep the ball. I take responsibility. This is me. I'm competitive. All my life, I've had to fight to realise my dream. So, I dribble to win.

"It's the fruition of daily work in training with Sir Alex Ferguson and Carlos Queiroz, our coach at United, and of the time I spent in the national team last summer with Luiz Felipe Scolari, who has also taught me a lot. It's not an explosion; it's a move towards maturity, a normal progression. Each day, I'm becoming a little bit more adult and I'm lucky to grow in a team that plays well at the moment. I have an objective in mind: to improve my output in the game, particularly in front of the goal. Ferguson and Scolari have equally played a key role in the way I have simplified my game.

"I try to be relaxed, natural, to improve, to become a better footballer. In this respect, the World Cup has given me a lot, particularly with the knockout games against the Netherlands

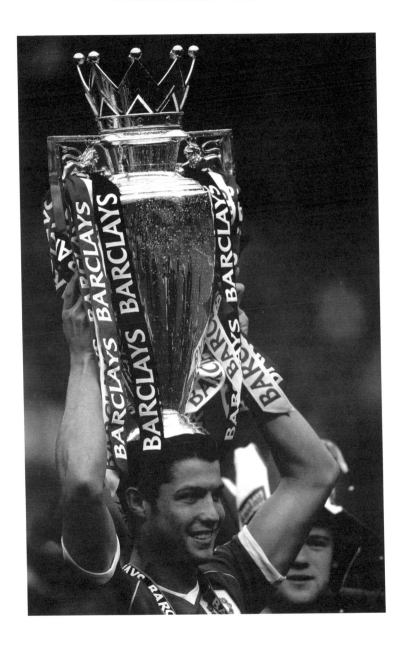

and England."

Ronaldo was born CRISTIANO RONALDO DOS SANTOS AVEIRO, with Ronaldo included because his father liked the laid-back style of the American President and actor, Ronald Reagan. The admiration extended to his parents calling his sister, a singer, Ronalda.

Now he says he carries the name of Ronaldo with pride and it's his preferred choice for the back of his football shirt, even though there is a clash of name with the equally famous Brazilian star Ronaldo.

Our Ronaldo didn't find his early days in Portugal very easy. He had been born and brought up in Funchal in Madeira and shipping him off to the big city of Lisbon to join Sporting found him mocked and teased. It must have been a bit like a lad from the depths of Lancashire going to London to join a big-city club like Arsenal, full of confident Cockneys.

Certainly there is a provocative style to his game, an arrogance suggesting perhaps that he is now a man out to make up for what he suffered as a youngster, looking for revenge, a player who is going to delight in humiliating opponents, or as *L'Equipe* suggests, therapy through dribbling. Ronaldo denies that he is deliberately trying to be provocative and says:

"In life, you have to follow your ideas through. And in the game, my football is defined by dribbling. I'm a winger. I have to face head-on opposition with a defender who I need to eliminate. I like this challenge. Some players might think that my way to dribble past is a bit provocative and that I look to excite the crowds, but this isn't the way I see it. In Manchester, everybody likes my game! Outside, OK, people criticise me, sometimes they whistle at me, but I don't give a damn."

Cristiano admits though that he found his early days frustrating, so much so that Sporting at one point brought his mother over from Madeira to Lisbon to give him more support.

He started playing organised football when he was eight for his local team, Andorinha, where his father was kit man. After a couple of seasons he moved to Madeira's biggest club Nacional and then when he was aged 11 Sporting took him for a £1500 fee to Lisbon and installed him in one of their nursery clubs, Alcochete, which was when the going got tough.

He was mocked for his Madeiran provincial accent. Looking back he says: "It wasn't easy to leave my family and my Madeira island to go to Lisbon and join Sporting. I came from a small island, not from Porto or another big city. And I arrived alone. To see a guy turning up from Madeira was not something normal for the others. Where I come from, it is very rare that footballers have this opportunity.

"It was as if I was speaking a foreign language! In Portugal, accents differ from one area to another, but the Madeira accent, blimey! When I arrived, absolutely everybody laughed at me. Today, I know that this is understandable, but when I was 11 or 12, well, I reacted badly. It really was a rough time.

"I was shy, and when people took the mickey, I would get worked up, I would become awfully angry. It's not good but it helped me later on. Today, I have such weaponry against bad times! I did stay five years on my own in Lisbon. My family only came to visit me from time to time. I therefore had to make my mark for people to accept me. I'm still young, but my maturity came very early on. Thanks to this experience as a kid exposed to the world of professionals and that of adults, inside I feel far older. Sometimes I was afraid, but it has never taken over my beliefs. I had a dream to realise. I wanted to be a great footballer. And today, I'm at Manchester United."

Although Cristiano had his problems as a youngster it did not stop his progress in football. At Sporting he played for the U16 team, the U17s, U18s, the B team and the first team all in the same season.

His appearance for Portugal in the World U17 Championships

brought him to the attention of some of Europe's leading clubs as an outstanding prospect. Manchester United started to monitor him and stepped up their interest after he had impressed their players with his display against them in a pre-season friendly. All doubts were swept away and United happily paid the £12.24m fee in August 2003. Within a week he was making his United debut against Bolton Wanderers on the opening day of season 2003-04, and after coming on as a substitute with the Reds leading 1-0 he helped turn the game into a runaway 4-0 win.

United fans were impressed and another triumph for Sir Alex Ferguson as the fans wondered and worried how the void left by the departure of David Beckham to Real Madrid was going to be filled. Here was their answer, a player capable of wearing the No. 7 shirt with the aplomb of the other 'magnificent sevens' Beckham, Eric Cantona, Bryan Robson and George Best.

Ronaldo says he didn't ask for the No. 7 shirt. He wanted the 28 that he had worn at Sporting but his new manager insisted he took the seven and says that right from the second game, people came up to him and said: 'Eh, do you know the number you're wearing? Do you know who wore it before you?'

He adds: "But I don't feel I have a greater responsibility because I wear No. 7. Whatever my number, I must give my best for my colours. Yes, it's quite a line-up. I'm honoured to belong to this list. History will judge if I'm worthy of it. Each one of them was a special player."

Four years hence, I think we already have a good idea that Cristiano Ronaldo is going to be worthy of joining the magnificent sevens. Sir Alex Ferguson has never had any doubts and halfway through his first season after a particularly impressive display in a 3-2 win over Everton he was purring: "There were some tough tackles going in on the lad but he had a fantastic game. He really showed what he is all about. He is still only 18 years old and that's why we are using him sparingly, but in a couple of years he'll be a truly outstanding player and we are thrilled by him."

Ronaldo marked his first season at Old Trafford with an FA Cup medal by scoring and helping to beat Millwall in the final, and Sir Alex was now even more enthusiastic about his prodigy.

"He is only 19 but he is sensational. Manchester United have always known how to make room for exceptional talents. Remember Bobby Charlton and George Best? I have learned, too, you always have to let the players express themselves. For a manager, a player like Ryan Giggs for example is a gift from heaven. It was the same thing with Eric Cantona. He would never have become the great player he was if I had not encouraged him to develop his talent. I think we were the perfect club for him. A club where he could puff out his chest and say 'I'm the boss here, I'm the king'. He has that aura, that presence, that faith in himself and it's the same with Ronaldo. Never stop him dribbling past opponents, because it's just that which makes him the player you want.

"A manager always has to be able to adapt what he says to each type of player. He'll say to some 'play it simple, you are never better than when you strip your game down.' Then there are others who can raise their game to a new level, one I can't conceive because I don't have their vision and because they see things that I, as their manager, can't see.

"Ronaldo will be one of those players, I'm sure, just like Cantona before him."

His first season also saw him make his debut for Portugal, playing in a 1-0 win against Kazakhstan before going on to help Portugal to the final of the 2004 European Championships, where they lost to Greece. Since then Cristiano has added to his international reputation, playing in the team that reached the World Cup quarter-finals after beating England, and at the time of writing he has scored 17 goals from 46 appearances, as well as causing general mayhem among the opposition.

Meanwhile his career at Old Trafford has continued apace, though there were some testing moments even before the winking episode in Germany. His father died in September 2005, the following month came the false rape allegations, he was banned for rudely gesturing at Benfica fans in the Champions League in Lisbon and he was sent off in the Manchester derby. I guess winning the Carling Cup was scant compensation for what he admitted had been a difficult time during the 2005-06 season.

There was also a crisis over his future with the rumour mill working overtime suggesting that Real Madrid and Barcelona were waiting to pounce. In the November, though, he signed a two-year contract extension to take him up to 2010 and said: "United have supported me all the way, they have stood by me and I want to repay them. I will repay the faith."

Inevitably though, given the player's increasing impact on the game, interest from Europe's big clubs just wouldn't go away and after the World Cup and the clash with Wayne Rooney the issue of his future surfaced again. During the January transfer window in 2007 reports claiming that Real Madrid were preparing a massive £35m bid prompted Sir Alex to insist that the player was not for sale at any price.

The temperature rose when Ronaldo's agent, Jorge Mendes, was pictured sitting next to Barcelona's director of football, but Fergie insisted: "The boy is happy here and everything is fine. He's at a good football club and he knows that. He's having a fantastic season and I don't think there is a better player in the world at the moment. He can realise all his potential and achieve everything he wants to do in his career here."

Nevertheless, United supporters breathed easier when the club proudly announced in the April that they had agreed terms on a new five-year contract to keep the player at the club until at least June 2012.

The manager declared: "It is fantastic news, it emphasises

the point that Cristiano is at the right club. He has a great relationship with the team, staff and the fans and he will go on to be one of Manchester United's greatest players."

Sir Bobby Charlton, no stranger to great players, says he sees abilities in Ronaldo that he has not seen before.

"It takes great players to grab the bull by the horns and lift people and he has been doing that recently. He does things I have never seen anyone else do. And he is as tough as hell. If you clatter him it doesn't bother him too much, he'll carry on. I think he has been a better player than even people here at Old Trafford realise."

The season ended in triumph with the Premier League title taken off Chelsea after three blank seasons, and it was undoubtedly the infusion of new young players like Ronaldo, Wayne Rooney and Nemanja Vidic to bolster the likes of Ryan Giggs, Paul Scholes and Rio Ferdinand that not only put United back on top but gives them every hope of staying there.

The plaudits flowed and Ronaldo was feted with awards...and quite rightly so because the player with tricks has matured and is now a team man in the real meaning of the word.

As Rene Meulensteen, the club's technical skills coach, explains: "At the end of Cristiano's first season with United I said he was the most talented, technically-gifted player at the club in terms of tricks. All he needed to do was become effective with his skills, and that's the transition he has made this season.

"What top attacking players possess at the highest level is a certain degree of unpredictability. That's what I have talked to him about. If he gets the ball and always starts to run with it then the defender gets wise to it. It's the same the other way, if he always passes it. So it's about getting the right package and having the ability to use all these skills for the right reasons, which is to create the right situation – crossing, shooting etc.

"In that respect he's made tremendous strides forward. He

knows that every time he steps on a pitch, he's going to make an impact. Because of what he has created already, defenders step off him. That means he's already created the time and space to run, and suddenly one key pass can do the trick.

"He's fast becoming the best player in the world. He's got the same attributes as Ronaldinho, a complete range of skills and attributes. I asked him what his aim was and he said he wanted to win plenty of prizes with the team and be the best player in the world. That's good – if you're going to have a dream it might as well be a big one! I asked him where he thought he was on a scale of 1-10 towards reaching that goal and he wasn't sure. I told him I thought he was an eight. If he can add bits to his game then nine and 10 will come very quickly.

"It's his attitude that I like about him. He has got the mentality that he can always add to his game. He never gets complacent and he wants to quicken his footwork. Skills development is about having a tool; wherever the defender is, on your left side or right side coming from the front or behind, you need to have certain things to help create a better situation. He's a quick boy, a very intelligent learner. He's always trying new things."

Cristiano Ronaldo might be the new kid on the block but at his present rate of progress he is going to make me wonder why I ever hesitated about including him in my Perfect 10.

CRISTIANO RONALDO - CAREER STATS

BORN:	Funchal, Madeira
DATE OF BIRTH:	February 5 1985
JOINED UNITED:	August 2003
UNITED LEAGUE APPS:	129
GOALS:	35
INT. CAPS (Portugal):	46
GOALS:	17

ALSO AVAILABLE IN THE SERIES